Facets Gay & Lesbian Video Guide

SECOND EDITION, REVISED AND EXPANDED

Revised and expanded by
GABRIEL GOMEZ

Original edition compiled by
PATRICK Z. McGAVIN

Facets Multi-Media, Inc./Academy Chicago Publishers

This book is respectfully dedicated in memoriam to Vito Russo, Stephen Harvey, Jay Scott and Parker Tyler.

Contents

Acknowledgments

The revised and expanded second edition of the *Facets Gay & Lesbian Video Guide* was edited by Catherine Foley and Milos Stehlik, with the able assistance of Hope Anne Nathan and Pamela Masco. For stills and permission to reproduce them, we thank First Run Features, Diamond Eye Productions, Fox-Lorber Home Video, World Artists, Something Weird Video, MPI, MGM, Circle Associates, Giorno Video, Orion Home Video, Meredian Video, Wolfe Video, HomeVision, Insider Video/Award Films International, Turner/New Line, Cinevista Video, Warner Home Video, Glitter Goddess Video, Live Entertainment, Video Active Releasing, Lucky Charms Studios, Columbia Tri-Star, Video Artists International, Interama, Xenon, Leora Films, MCA/Universal, Kino International and Water Bearer Films.

Upfront

This book is a response to the home video revolution; it is a guide to the growing number of available videotapes on gay and lesbian themes. Although many of these tapes still remain outside the mainstream of commercial distribution, this too, is changing. A result of this exciting development is that you no longer need to live in a major urban area with its own gay and lesbian film festival to see lesbian or gay films. All of the films in this guide are available for home viewing on video cassette or laser disc.

Audiences for gay and lesbian cinema are continually growing as gay and lesbian films gain broader distribution. As a result, an increasing number of filmmakers are able to make larger-budget gay- and lesbian-themed films. This evolution is reflected in the films which are described in the *Facets Gay & Lesbian Video Guide*: we progress from features which "dared" to have a token gay character to films in which a filmmaker is free to explore issues of gay and lesbian sexuality, relationships and personal dynamics.

This guide is not a history of gay and lesbian cinema. Our approach is consumer-based—we concentrated only on films which are available and accessible on tape or laser disc. You can do more than read about these films: you can view them. There are many, many more gay and lesbian films which have never been shown or distributed in the United States or released on video. As the market grows, undoubtedly many more of these now "classic" works will be released.

There are also many documentaries, films and videos on gay and lesbian issues which are distributed through the nontheatrical or educational marketplace. These can be rented for public or educational screenings, but are not included in the *Facets Gay & Lesbian Video Guide* because they are not readily accessible to the consumer. Again, as the so-called "non-fiction" film gains greater acceptance within the home video marketplace, more and more of these works will become available and accessible at home video prices and in video stores throughout the country.

Finally, we excluded pornography; those who want to see it know where and how to get it.

Our approach in this guide has been cinematic; we focused on each tape's artistic or dramatic film values. A number of the tapes included in the *Facets Gay & Lesbian Video Guide* are without overt gay or lesbian content - some of the work of Rainer W. Fassbinder, Pier Paolo Pasolini, Chantal Akerman, Sergei Paradjanov, Tennesee Williams or Luchino Visconti, for example. We felt it was important to be comprehensive and inclusive—to write about the "body of work" of these key figures of gay and lesbian cinema so that their work can be appreciated in all its richness.

There are obviously many other great figures of cinema history whose homosexuality came to be more widely known years after their deaths—the cinema pioneer Sergei Eisenstein, the brilliant German Expressionist filmmaker Friedrich Murnau, the pioneer of the documentary, Basil Wright—are just three examples. In all these cases, no work of theirs directly or indirectly touches upon their own sexual orientation.

There are more male-gay than lesbian tapes in this guide. This is an unfortunate reflection of the male-centeredness of the international film industry. It's a situation which is also finally beginning to change; we can only hope that more and more talented women are able to get the financing and creative control to make the films they want to make.

Perhaps most refreshing is the number of contemporary gay and lesbian filmmakers who now have an entire body of work that is informed by a gay or lesbian sensibility. These include American independents Gregg Araki, Gus Van Sant and Barbara Hammer; Spanish filmmakers Eloy de la Iglesia and Pedro Almodovar; Germany's Monika Treut and Rosa von Praunheim; and British director Stephen Frears.

We welcome your comments, and sincerely wish this guide allows you to spend many enjoyable hours watching what these dozens of talented filmmakers have accomplished.

Where To Buy or Rent Tapes

An increasing number of video stores throughout the country are venturing outside the hit-driven mentality and stock foreign and independent features and documentaries.

If your video store is not one of these progressive outlets, you can purchase any tape or laser disc in this book which is currently in print directly from Facets Video. To order, within the United States call toll-free at 800-331-6197, e-mail to sales@facets.org or fax to 773-929-5437. Otherwise, call 773-281-9075. Or write: Facets Video, 1517 West Fullerton Avenue, Chicago, Illinois 60614. The "S" numbers at the end of each video description in this book refer to Facets Video's sales order numbers.

Facets Video also offers a rent-by-mail service within the continental United States. For rent-by-mail membership information, call 800-5-FACETS (800-532-2387), FAX at 773-929-5437 or write Facets Video Rentals, 1517 West Fullerton Avenue, Chicago, Illinois 60614.

Prices

The prices listed in this book were current at the time of publication. However, video and laser disc prices are volatile and do change at the drop of a hat. Fortunately, this most often means that they are substantially reduced.

Out of Print Tapes and Laser Discs

Much like the volatile price changes of home video and laser discs, tapes and discs go in and out of print with increasing frequency. Licensing rights expire, video companies shift direction or go out of business. Many tapes which go out of print later reappear on another label, often in a better (enhanced) version. Video stores which purchased copies of the out-of-print tape before it went out of print continue to rent those tapes.

Format

Tapes in BETA format: Although BETA is still around and has its ardent core of often vocal supporters, it is very difficult to rent or buy tapes in BETA format. If you are determined to stay only with the BETA format, it's a good idea to join one of the BETA collector's clubs.

Laser Disc Availability: An increasing number of titles are available on laser disc, often in "enhanced" versions (widescreen, with additional material like director's notes or comments). Unfortunately, some laser disc manufacturers actually press discs only when they get enough orders to warrant the pressing. This means that if you're trying to purchase other-than-mainstream titles, you may have to wait a while to get the laser disc you want. Hopefully this situation will improve with time as the superior image and sound quality of laser discs gain popularity, and as laser disc prices drop.

To Order Additional Copies of This Book

To order additional copies of this book, you may call toll-free: 800-331-6197, or write: Facets Video, 1517 West Fullerton Avenue, Chicago, Illinois 60614. Enclose $12.95 plus $2 shippping and handling.

Facets Gay & Lesbian Video Guide

1988

A lurid and bizarre rumination on celebrity and spectacle, *1988* concerns a dying librarian who enlists a group of untalented performers in her bid to remake *Showboat* as a musical comedy. With Ed Nylund, Skip Kovington, Carolyn Zaremba and Willie Boy Walker. The film "mixes deadly seriousness and high camp, avant-garde aesthetics and transsexual athletics with an atmosphere that is alternately sordid and seductive" (David Harris, *Boston Phoenix*).
VHS: S01625. $59.95.
Richard Schmidt, USA, 1977, 93 mins.

27 Pieces of Me

In this bold independent feature, Tanya (Tina M. Henning), a lesbian sculptor, is forced to confront her sister Ramona (Angelique von Halle) when she arrives on her doorstep unannounced. Both women have been having relationship troubles. Fortunately, Tanya's roommate Bold (Jonathan Harris) helps the two women begin a rapprochement that they so desperately need and want.
VHS: S27479. $39.95.
Gerald Donohoe, USA, 1995, 90 mins.

The 4th Man

Paul Verhoeven's gothic thriller is adapted from gay writer Gerard Reve's story about an Amsterdam novelist (Jeroen Krabbe) racked by mysterious, homoerotic dreams. The novelist's feverish dream images are somehow connected to his relationship with Christine (Renee Soutendijk), an enigmatic, thrice-widowed social climber. The writer seduces Christine's fiancé (Thom Hoffman), setting in motion a harrowing conclusion. Screenplay by Gerard Soeteman. Cinematography by Jan De Bont. With Dolf De Vries and Geert De Jong. English dubbed.
VHS: S00461. $24.95.
Paul Verhoeven, Holland, 1984, 104 mins.

ABC Stage 67: Truman Capote's A Christmas Memory

Geraldine Page and Donnie Melvin star in this dramatic television adaptation of Capote's autobiographical account of his youth during the depression in the South. Living on severely limited means with his dotty cousin, a ten-year-old Capote was enriched by singular experiences. In this film, the baking of Christmas fruitcakes for relatives becomes the center of warm and involved undertaking. 51 mins.
VHS: S29527. $19.95.

Absolutely Fabulous

Jennifer Saunders and Joanna Lumley made this irreverent BBC comedy series a smash hit with their scathingly funny impersonations of bored, dumb, wealthy London women. Edina and Patsy bring excess to new levels of absurdity. This set includes all 18 episodes and a 30-minute behind-the-scenes look at the show hosted by Saunders, which also features priceless outtakes.
VHS: S29989. $99.98.

Abuse

A young boy, abused by his parents, finally discovers some much needed emotional gratification when he becomes the focus of a documentary called *Abuse*. He becomes close to the gay man directing this film. Shot in a documentary style, this film raises tough questions about the nature of intimacy between an adult man and a 14-year-old boy.
VHS: S28068. $79.95.
Arthur J Bresson, USA, 1995, 93 mins.

Accatone

Pier Paolo Pasolini's debut film deals with a world he knew well: the streets of Rome's slums and the lives of thieves, prostitutes and junkies. *Accatone* is the portrait of a young hustler (Franco Citti) who can't quite cut it as a pimp. With the police on his trail, he faces the choice of working for minimal wages or turning to stealing. "[The film's] rough-edged style, its cool, unhysterical portrayal of corruption, cruelty, and violence, and its quiet lyricism marked one of the most significant directorial debuts of the sixties" (Georges Sadoul). Cinematography by Tonino Delli Colli. With Silvana Corsini, Franca Pasut, Roberto Scaringella and Adele Cambria. Italian with English subtitles.

VHS: S11153. $39.95.

Pier Paolo Pasolini, Italy, 1961, 120 mins.

The Adjuster

The hypnotic fourth feature by Toronto-based filmmaker Atom Egoyan deals with his recurring themes of the omnipresence of video, voyeurism, fractured nuclear families and gay and straight sexual domination. Three interwoven stories are crosscut: Noah is an insurance adjuster who manipulates and controls clients who have lost their property; his wife Hera is a government film censor who surreptitiously records the offending material on video; and an ex-football player and his twisted wife play out elaborate sexual games on the unsuspecting. With Elias Koteas, Arsinee Khanjian and Maury Chaykin.

VHS: S18458. $19.98.

Atom Egoyan, Canada, 1991, 102 mins.

Adventures of Picasso

A madcap slapstick piece about a group of actors who impersonate major writers and artists, including Picasso, Dali and Apollinaire. The film's central relationship examines the bond between Gertrude Stein and Alice B. Toklas. With Gosta Ekman, Hans Alfredson and Margaretha Krook. Swedish with English subtitles.

VHS: S02118. Currently out of print. May be available for rental in some video stores.

Tage Danielsson, Sweden, 1978, 92 mins.

Anita, Dances of Vice

Advise and Consent

Otto Preminger's political drama, in which an accusation of homosexuality, blackmail, suicide and scandal follow the President's appointment of an unpopular Secretary of State, is a kind of catharsis of 1950s McCarthyist paranoia. But the film remains a powerful melodrama with skillful performances from Henry Fonda, Charles Laughton, Burgess Meredith and Peter Lawford.

VHS: S01994. $29.95.
Otto Preminger, USA, 1962, 142 mins.

A.I.D.S.C.R.E.A.M., Ecce Homo and Final Solutions

Three short experimental films by gay filmmaker Jerry Tartaglia are joined on this video. Along with *A.I.D.S.C.R.E.A.M.*, *Ecco Homo* and *Final Solutions*, these works explore fear, rage, the anti-sex and anti-gay movements, and even the rise of AIDS consumerism. It's an angry, arrogant and unapologetic collection.

VHS: S27222. $59.95.

Akermania, Volume One

A collection of short works from the gifted Belgian director Chantal Akerman, whose early work was heavily influenced by the avant-garde, anti-narrative bent of Canadian filmmaker Michael Snow, American independent Stan Brakhage and French/Swiss director Jean-Luc Godard. Her early films explore real time, self-definition and sexual identities. Akerman plays the lead role in her first film, *Saute Ma Ville* (1968). The program includes *I'm Hungry, I'm Cold*, a story of two Belgian girls set loose in Paris, and *Hotel Monterey* (1972), an experimental silent work set around the New York hotel. French with English subtitles.

VHS: S16298. $19.98.
Chantal Akerman, France/Belgium, 89 mins.

Ali: Fear Eats the Soul

Rainer Werner Fassbinder's reconsideration of Douglas Sirk's *All That Heaven Allows* captures the complicated social and racial configurations of West German society. The narrative unravels the doom-laden affair of an older German floor washer (Brigitte Mira) and an inarticulate Moroccan mechanic (El Hadi Ben Salem) half her age. The film studies her family's violent opposition to their relationship. A

visually flamboyant work, *Ali: Fear Eats the Soul* is alternately a moving romance, a social comedy and an incisive study of racial prejudice. With Barbara Valentin, Irm Hermann and Peter Gauhe. Cinematography by Jurgen Jurges. German with enhanced English subtitles.
VHS: S11590. $79.95.
Rainer W. Fassbinder, W. Germany, 1974, 94 mins.

Aliens Cut My Hair

An extravagantly campy video by Michael McIntosh based on Gentry Johnson's surreal comic strip Fabulous Space Stories. The story unfolds in a dreamy outer space populated by hairdressers and alien transvestites who travel in a vibrator-shaped space ship. When a young ensign shows insufficient appreciation for a haircut, the outraged hairdresser vows eternal revenge. "Every bit as campy as it sounds" (Steven Miller, *Seattle Gay News*).
VHS: S18918. $39.95.

American Avant-Garde Films

A collection of five experimental American films from 1906-1933. Of particular note is James Watson and Melville Webber's *Lot in Sodom* (1933), an experimental depiction of Old Testament stories told with an explicit homosexual content. Also interesting is *Salome*, a highly stylized version of Oscar Wilde's play with the gifted dancer Nazimova, adapted from drawings by Aubrey Beardsley. Other titles in this compilation are Edwin S. Porter's *Dream of a Rarebit Fiend*, Watson and Webber's *The Fall of the House of Usher* and Charles Vidor's *The Bridge*.
VHS: S09927. $49.95.

American Fabulous

This is a highly regarded American independent work featuring the strange and hypnotic recollections of a nomadic, itinerant writer. He reflects on fabulous adventures that span a wide swath of the U.S. ranging from his small town home to New York and Los Angeles. It's a "tour of a wild, low-life gay existence [that's] captivating, hilarious, yet touching. Jeffrey Strouth displays a wit that might conceivably amuse Oscar Wilde" (Kevin Thomas, *Los Angeles Times*).
VHS: S18413. $29.95.
Reno Dakota, USA, 1992, 105 mins.

Aliens Cut My Hair

The American Soldier

Rainer Werner Fassbinder's cryptic, self-reflexive homage to Hollywood gangster films is an existential, absurdist film with a bleak center. The story follows an American expatriate (Karl Scheydt) who returns to Munich after serving a tour in Vietnam. His fragile inner state is exploited by the police, who program him into a dispassionate assassin. "The film marks a decisive step towards 'real' Fassbinder: the absurdity of its world of second-hand experience invests every cliche with a meaning it never had before" (*Time Out*). Cinematography by Dietrich Lohmann and Herbert Pajzold. With Elga Sorbas, Jan George, Margarethe von Trotta and Kurt Raab. German with English subtitles.
VHS: S16498. $29.95.
Rainer W. Fassbinder, W. Germany, 1970, 80 mins.

Amor Bandido

Bruno Barreto's unsentimental, stark realization of a tabloid account of a frightened prostitute and dancer (Cristina Ache) who is brutalized by her father and drawn into the psychotic lair of an impassioned, stone-faced serial killer (Paulo Guarnieri). Bleak and riveting. Male prostitution figures prominently in a sub-plot. Portuguese with English subtitles.
VHS: S12945. $19.98.
Bruno Barreto, Brazil, 1979, 95 mins.

Andy Warhol

An impressionistic and freewheeling documentary portrait of the seminal American artist, filmmaker and cult figure whose verve, talent and finely tuned gift for welding commerce and iconography established the tenets of pop art and Americana. The film is an intriguing collection of conversations with Warhol's associates and friends who discuss his family, art and work. 78 mins.

VHS: S07604. $39.95.

Kim Evans, Great Britain, 1987, 79 mins.

Andy Warhol/Keith Haring

A pair of documentaries on two of the most intriguing figures in the pop art movement. *Andy Warhol: Made in China* studies the activities of Warhol and his friends during a 1985 expedition to mainland China. *Drawing the Line: A Portrait of Keith Haring* investigates the relationship between Haring's art and its social and political context.

Laser: LD70833. Currently out of print. May be available for rental in some video stores.

Andy Warhol: The Scope of His Art

This insightful program explores the ways in which Andy Warhol's paintings, films and graphics are connected to his sensibility and working methods. 25 mins.

VHS: S09460. $174.00.

Andy Warhol's Bad

A strange, off-center meditation on the sickness and perversity of American society in the aftermath of '60s excesses. An anonymous Queens businesswoman (Carroll Baker) mounts an elaborate front, providing her clients beautiful, highly skilled, professional female assassins. The primary story concerns whether a weak man (Perry King) will go forth and kill an autistic child. It's a soap-opera vision of America, alternately horrifying and surreal. With Susan Tyrrel, Stefania Cassini and Cyrinda Foxe.

Laser: LD70832. Currently out of print. May be available for rental in some video stores.

Jed Johnson, USA, 1977, 107 mins.

Andy Warhol's Dracula

Andy Warhol's collaborator Paul Morrissey directed this eerie, camp version of Bram Stoker's novel. In Morrissey's version, the Count (played by Fassbinder regular Udo Kier) has left Romania for Italy in a desperate search for virgin blood. The movie is also known as *Blood for Dracula* and *Young Dracula*. The cast includes Joe Dallesandro, Arno Juerging and directors Vittorio De Sica and Roman Polanski.
VHS: S02301. $14.98.
Paul Morrissey, USA, 1974, 106 mins.

Andy Warhol's Frankenstein

Paul Morrissey's fiendishly bizarre interpretation of Mary Shelley's gothic novel finds a demented baron (Udo Kier) cloning freakish monsters out of human remains. "Severed limbs, gobs of livid human entrails, a hideously efficient decapitating gadget...are among the treats that slither off the screen.... The most outrageously gruesome epic ever unleashed" (Bruce Williamson, *Playboy*). With Joe Dallesandro, Monique Van Vooren and Srdjan Zelenovic.
VHS: S02302. $14.98.
Paul Morrissey, USA, 1973, 95 mins.

The Angelic Conversation

British filmmaker Derek Jarman's apocalyptic, fiery visualization of 12 Shakespeare sonnets read by actress Judi Dench. The film explores Jarman's characteristic themes and preoccupations: desire, longing, homoeroticism and the mystical. With Paul Reynolds and Phillip Williamson. "A hypnotically beautiful film" (*Time Out*).
VHS: S12677. $29.95.
Derek Jarman, Great Britain, 1985, 80 mins.

Anita, Dances of Vice

An aging woman believes she's the incarnation of Anita Berber, the notorious "naked" dancer of the Weimar Republic whose drug addiction, flagrant bisexuality and kinky behavior occasioned her social downfall. The police commit the woman to a mental institution where her dreams conjure up Anita's life. Anita combines an "exuberantly tacky expressionism and pornographic insolence. Huber is irresistibly funny as the city's pugnacious doyenne of sin" (J. Hoberman, *Village Voice*). German with English subtitles.
VHS: S09349. $39.95.
Rosa von Praunheim, W. Germany, 1987, 85 mins.

Another Way

Set against the backdrop of the 1956 Hungarian uprising, *Another Way* charts the tragic repercussions of a lesbian affair between two journalists. Livia, the beautiful, dissatisfied wife of an army officer, is drawn to Eva, a flamboyant, relentless reporter. This beautifully conceived, deftly acted film plunges into deeper issues of political and sexual repression. Cinematography by Tamas Andor. Jadwiga Jankowska-Cieslak won the Best Actress award at Cannes. Based on the autobiographical novel of co-screenwriter Erzsebet Galgoczi. With Grazyna Szapolowska and Jozef Kroner. Hungarian with English subtitles.

VHS: S14097. $59.95.
Karoly Makk, Hungary, 1982, 100 mins.

Another Country

Marek Kanievska adapts Julian Mitchell's play about social, sexual and political repression within Britain's academic elite. Constructed in flashbacks, the story is a provocative rumination on alienation. The film argues that oppressive social conditioning forced Guy Burgess and Donald Maclean, the main characters, to conceal their sexual orientation. Both ultimately ended up working as spies for the Soviet Union. With Rupert Everett, Colin Firth, Michael Jenn and Robert Addie.

VHS: S00060. Currently out of print. May be available for rental in some video stores.
Marek Kanievska, Great Britain, 1984, 90 mins.

Apart from Hugh

Collin and Hugh have been together for one year. A party commemorating this anniversary forces Collin to reconsider his feelings about their relationship. Commitment, growth, and above all, love, are the buzzwords in the air as these two men struggle with their feelings for each other.

VHS: S27613. $39.95.
Jon FitzGerald, USA, 1994, 87 mins.

Amor Bandido

Apartment Zero

Martin Donovan's atmospheric, homoerotic thriller is a probing account of desire and oppression. The film explores the strange relationship of a British-born Argentine repertory cinema owner (Colin Firth) and a handsome, enigmatic American stranger (Hart Bochner) who answers his advertisement for a sublet. Through long takes and a striking use of restricted space, Donovan creates an overwhelmingly mordant sense of claustrophobia, entrapment and sexual confinement. *Apartment Zero* is one of the best films about the unsettling influence of American political and cultural power in Latin America. With Dora Bryan, Liz Smith and Fabrizio Bentivolglio.

VHS: S11690. Currently out of print. May be available for rental in some video stores.
Laser: LD70842. Currently out of print. May be available for rental in some video stores.
Martin Donovan, Great Britain, 1989, 125 mins.

Arabian Nights

The final installment of Pier Paolo Pasolini's trilogy, following *The Decameron* and *The Canterbury Tales*, *Arabian Nights* interweaves ten stories of love, sex, desire and betrayal connected by one man's relentless search for his kidnapped slave girl. Pasolini's use of landscape, texture, culture and local color is profoundly lyrical. "Rich, romantic and magnificent. Its graphic sex scenes, which have a dreamy kind of beauty to them, are erotic without being pornographic" (Vincent Canby). Music by Ennio Morricone. With Ninetto Davoli, Franco Citti and Franco Merli. Italian with English subtitles.

VHS: S07021. $79.95.
Pier Paolo Pasolini, Italy, 1974, 130 mins.

Aria

Ten internationally acclaimed filmmakers direct ten "vignettes," each based on a famous operatic aria. Particularly notable are Julien Temple's interpretation of *Rigoletto* as a colorful sex farce; Ken Russell's *Turandot*, in which a beautiful young woman is disfigured in a car accident; and Derek Jarman's interpretation of "Depuis le jour" from Charpentier's *Louise*, a haunting super-8 piece which uses primitive, black and white, grainy visual stocks to achieve a feverish intensity. The cast(s) include Tilda Swinton, Bridget Fonda and Linzi Drew. Great Britain, 1987, 90 mins.

VHS: S07452. $14.98.

The Art of Cruising Men

From the creators of *Max Headroom* comes England's best-selling gay video of all time. This streetwise "video sex guide for the 21st century" traces how men cruise men from prehistoric times to the hedonistic clubs of the '90s. "One of the best gay videos on sale" (*The Pink Paper*). "Great...one brilliant, funny and well-produced video" (*QX Magazine*). VHS: S30149. $39.95.

Peter Litten, Great Britain, 1995, 70 mins.

As Is

An adaptation of William Hoffman's play about former lovers who are reunited when one of them, a talented writer, discovers he's stricken with AIDS. Their bonding transforms the writer's anger into cathartic relief and a quest for love and happiness. With Robert Carradine, Joanna Miles, Jonathan Hadary and Colleen Dewhurst. VHS: S03289. $19.98.

Michael Lindsay-Hogg, USA, 1986, 85 mins.

Ashik Kerib

The final film of the visionary Georgian director Sergei Paradjanov, *Ashik Kerib* is a lyrical, sublime mosaic about fortitude, desire and mystery. Loosely adapted from Mikhail Lermontov's magical tale *Arabian Nights*, the film concerns the odyssey of Ashik Kerib (Yuri Goyan), a wandering minstrel whose determination to marry a beautiful woman is overruled by her powerful merchant father. "What comes across is Paradjanov's love of music, dance and gorgeous costumes, and his identification with the misunderstood artist" (*The Faber Companion to Foreign Films*). Cinematography by Albert Yavuryan. With Yiur Mgoyan, Veronikia Metonidze and Levan Natroshvili. Azerbaijani and Georgian with English subtitles. VHS: S19055. $59.95.

Sergei Paradjanov, Russia, 1988, 78 mins.

Chantal Akerman (b. 1950) is a gifted stylist whose work radically incorporates the avant-garde and experimental within a highly personal method of expression. Born in Brussels, Akerman was inspired to make films after seeing Jean-Luc Godard's *Pierrot le Fou* (1965). In the late '60s, she attended the International University Theater in Paris. In 1969, Akerman directed her first short, *Saute Ma Ville*, which was followed two years later with *L'Enfant Aime*. In the early '70s, Akerman lived in New York's East Village, where she was influenced by the American avant-garde. "I saw the films of Michael Snow and Jonas Mekas—they opened my mind to many things—the relationship between film and your body [and] time as the most important thing in film.... Seeing their films gave me courage to try something else, not just to make money. Before I went to New York...I thought Bergman and Fellini were the greatest filmmakers. Not any more, because they are not dealing with time and space as the most important elements in film," Akerman said.

Akerman returned to Europe in 1973 and, beginning with *Je, Tu, Il, Elle* (1974), launched a new phase as a feature filmmaker. With this film, she developed her distinctive, minimalist visual style, one based on an exacting sense of composition and the use of long, unbroken takes. Akerman deliberately forsakes conventional narrative forms; her films are characterized by slow, deliberate pacing, spare dialogue and precise, stationary camera set-ups. Her compositions are elegantly crafted with subtle variations in light, tone and texture.

Akerman's breakthrough film is *Jeanne Dielman, 23 quai du Commerce, 1080 Bruxelles* (1975). Set over three days, the film painstakingly charts the daily activities of a woman who supports her son through a detached, almost casual form of prostitution. The film's use of real time "forces us to see how many steps are involved in each simple task. It also accentuates the central problem of boredom: Jeanne is not terrified by 'Time's winged chariot,' but the 'vast deserts of eternity' that threaten to engulf her," Marsha Kinder wrote in *Film Quarterly*. It could be argued that *Jeanne Dielman*, as all of Akerman's films, is informed by a clear feminist sensibility, but she has resisted that characterization.

Following *Jeanne Dielman*, Akerman directed *News from Home* (1976), *Les Rendezvous d'Anna* (1978) and *Toute Une Nuit* (1982). In describing Akerman's formally rigorous films, J. Hoberman wrote that she "designs films that interrogate the march of time in the form of narrative, playing with audience desire, thwarting even the most humble expectations, and providing an entirely unprecedented sort of pleasure." Akerman continued her investigations of different forms and subject matter with *The Eighties* (1986). The film is constructed in two parts, with the first hour shot on video and the last section—an opulent succession of musical numbers—shot on 35mm. *American Stories* (1988) is a collection of stories and anecdotes about Jewish immigrants in New York. *Nuit et jour* (1991) concerns a beautiful young woman who maintains two obsessive, simultaneous affairs. The same year, Akerman made *Contre l'oubli* (also known as *Against Oblivion* and *Ecrire contre l'oubli*).

Akerman's film *From the East* (1993) is a documentary essay that records her journey from the former East Germany to Moscow. In 1994, she co-wrote and directed *Portrait of a Young Girl at the End of the 1960s in Brussels*, which has been compared to Richard Linklater's *Before Sunrise*. It is the story of two people walking around a European city; unlike *Sunrise* they talk but never really connect. In 1996, Akerman both co-wrote and directed *Un Divan a New York*, starring Juliette Binoche and William Hurt. It is a romantic comedy revolving around psychoanalysis.

Window Shopping (written by Chantal Akerman)

B

Babette in "The Return of the Secret Society"

Babette is a hip, young sex kitten who has travelled the world and is now settling down in New York City. In need of employment, she returns to her former career in "the secret society," a world of mail-order porn and prostitution. She quickly befriends Ramon, a kinky photographer, and finds herself drawn to Carla, one of his favorite models. Together, Carla and Babette pose for Ramon and his camera, initiate a new member into the secret society via a far-out candlelight orgy, and join a group of horny young housewives called the Daughters of Lesbos. Very rare sleaze from the 1960s. With Claudia Cheer, Jo Sweet, Carla Costa and Sue Akers.
VHS: S27628. $19.98.
Peter Woodcock, USA, 1968, 80 mins.

Baby Doll

Elia Kazan's lurid, Southern gothic about a grotesque romantic triangle. The sexual intrigue is unleashed by a shrewd businessman (Eli Wallach) who insinuates himself into the lives of two dirt-poor Southerners, Karl Malden and his nymphet wife, Carroll Baker. Wallach's presence opens up primal feelings of seduction, repression, jealousy and loss. Adapted from two short one-act plays by Tennessee Williams, the film deals with the writer's characteristic themes and was condemned upon its release by the Catholic Legion of Decency. With Mildred Dunnock, Lonny Chapman and Rip Torn.
VHS: S00085. $19.98.
Elia Kazan, USA, 1956, 115 mins.

The Balcony

In this adaptation of Jean Genet's famous play, Madame Irma (Shelley Winters) rules a brothel during the anarchy and social rupture of a violent revolution. The interlocking stories dovetail when the police chief (Peter Falk) who tries to suppress the revolution and the leader (Leonard Nimoy) of the revolutionaries confront one another in the brothel. Lee Grant gives a powerful performance as Winters' lesbian confidante. The film deftly melds a surreal edge to the play's allegorical texture. Cinematography by George Folsey. With Peter Brocco, Ruby Dee and Kent Smith.
VHS: S09554. $29.95.
Joseph Strick, USA, 1963, 87 mins.

Babette in "The Return of the Secret Society"

Ballot Measure 9

This winner of the Special Jury Award at Sundance in 1995 follows the fight around Oregon's Ballot Measure 9. Essentially, the initiative would have denied lesbians and gay men civil rights protection. Though defeated, it was the center of acrimonious debate and tense standoffs. This documentary captures the heroic spirit of the people who stood up against bigotry, even under threat of physical harm.

VHS: S27476. $29.98.

Heather MacDonald, USA, 1995, 72 mins.

Basileus Quartet

A literate, intelligent work about the profound changes which confront the aging members of a string quartet who suffer the death of one of their members, a violinist. His replacement is young and brash and the artists are at first taken aback by his vitality and exuberance. The young violinist also challenges the players' sexual attitudes, especially their homoerotic attraction to him. Music by Schubert, Beethoven, Haydn. English dubbed.

VHS: S00099. Currently out of print. May be available for rental in some video stores.
Laser: LD70860. Currently out of print. May be available for rental in some video stores.

Fabio Carpi, Italy/France, 1984, 105 mins.

Beautiful Dreamers

Rip Torn delivers a stunning performance as Walt Whitman in this drama about a young doctor who encounters hostile reactions from the citizens of his small community when he befriends the poet; Whitman's philosophy of sexual liberation is at odds with the conservative climate of his times. With Colm Feore, Wendel Meldrum, Sheila McCarthy and Colin Fox.

VHS: S17443. Currently out of print. May be available for rental in some video stores.

John Kent Harrison, Great Britain, 1991, 108 mins.

Beautiful Mystery

Shinohara is a young bodybuilder who joins a para-military sect in Northern Japan. Amidst the discipline and rigor of the group, his instructor, Takizawa, develops a special interest in this new recruit. Before long, they develop a special and loving relationship. Japanese with English subtitles.

VHS: S29952. $39.95.

Nakamura Genji, Japan, 1983, 60 mins.

Beauty and the Beast

Jean Cocteau's superb adaptation of Marie Leprince de Beaumont's dark fairy tale is a ferociously inventive depiction of erotic obsession, as a young woman discovers a tender soul beneath a monstrous beast. The film's visual style is sculpted and heavily influenced by the Flemish painter Vermeer. Rene Clement is credited as co-director, though this delirious achievement was largely Cocteau's. "A sensuously fascinating film, the visual progression of the fable into a dream-world casts its unpredictable spell" (Bosley Crowther). With Jean Marais, Josette Day and Marcel Andre. Cinematography by Henri Alekan. French with English subtitles.

VHS: S00110. $24.95.
Laser: Cocteau, CAV. LD70865. $89.95.

Jean Cocteau, France, 1946, 90 mins.

Becket

A powerful work on the conflict between church and state, Peter Glenville's naturalistic adaptation of Jean Anouilh's play dramatizes the complicated friendship of Henry II (Richard Burton) and Thomas Becket (Peter O'Toole). Becket's quick ascension from chancellor to archbishop threatens Henry's power and moral authority, altering the nature of their friendship and eventually forcing its violent disruption. Cinematography by Geoffrey Unsworth. Music by Laurence Rosenthal. With Donald Wolfit, John Gielgud, Martita Hunt and Pamela Brown.

VHS: S02638. $59.95.
Laser: LD70866. Currently out of print. May be available for rental in some video stores.
Peter Glenville, Great Britain, 1964, 149 mins.

Beethoven's Nephew

Former Warhol protege Paul Morrissey directed this stylish investigation of unrequited love and erotic obsession, based on Ludwig van Beethoven's sexual attraction to his nephew Karl, who violently rejected the composer's advances. "Full of homoerotic nuances" (Vincent Canby, *The New York Times*).

VHS: S08089. $19.95.
Laser: LD70868. $39.95.
Paul Morrissey, 1988, 103 mins.

Before Stonewall

A revealing and award-winning documentary, this film offers an effective and accurate history of the gay and lesbian liberation movement. In a quiet, funny and perceptive manner, directors Greta Schiller and Robert Rosenberg celebrate the flair and unbending determination of various gay and lesbian pioneers, honoring their struggles. The filmmakers chart the formation of the movement through memoirs, anecdotes, interviews, archival footage and home movies.

VHS: S11587. Currently out of print. May be available for rental in some video stores.
Greta Schiller/Robert Rosenberg, USA, 1985, 87 mins.

Ballot Measure 9

Being at Home with Claude

French-Canadian director Jean Beaudin's shocking work is adapted from Rene-Daniel Dubois' play. The film delves into the violent relations between two radically different men: Yves, a casual thrill seeker and prostitute, and Claude, a writer and student from a socially prominent family. Yves kills Claude in a fit of passion. Taking the form of an interrogation, the film—using icy black-and-white flashbacks—tries to penetrate Yves' mind to understand the roots of the crime. "The film succeeds in bringing us all to a universal precipice and invites us to peer momentarily into the lonely void of an unimaginable future" (Toronto Film Festival). Cinematography by Thomas Vamos. With Roy Dupuis, Jacques Godin, Jean-Francois Pichette and Gaston Lepage. French with English subtitles.

VHS: S19441. Currently out of print. May be available for rental in some video stores.

Jean Beaudin, Canada, 1991, 85 mins.

Bellissima

In Luchino Visconti's third feature, set in a grim, claustrophobic Rome, the flamboyant Anna Magnani plays a poor, crafty woman determined that her daughter will win a child-star competition organized by Cinecitta studios. Problems ensue when Magnani becomes disillusioned by the process. "It rivals most Hollywood-on-Hollywood movies in ironic entertainment value" (*Time Out*). Cinematography by Piero Portalupi and Paul Ronald. With Walter Chiari, Tina Apicella and Alessandro Blasetti. Italian with English subtitles.

VHS: S00116. $59.95.

Luchino Visconti, Italy, 1951, 113 mins.

Berlin Affair

Liliana Cavani adapts Hanns Zischler's *The Buddhist Crisis*, in this portrait of prewar Nazi Germany. The story captures the lesbian relationship between a dissatisfied diplomat's wife (Gudrun Landgrebe) and the daughter (Mio Takaki) of a Japanese ambassador. The troubles start when Louise's husband learns about the affair. With Kevin McNally, Massimo Girotti and Philippe Leroy.

VHS: S04953. Currently out of print. May be available for rental in some video stores.

Liliana Cavani, Italy/W. Germany, 1985, 96 mins.

Becket

The Best Man

Homosexuality is the skeleton in the closet in this political exposé of corruption in Washington. Henry Fonda plays the liberal Senator Russell and Cliff Robertson his rival, Senator Cantwell, who hides a youthful indiscretion in his past. Gore Vidal wrote the screenplay. With terrific performances from Edie Adams, Margaret Leighton, Ann Sothern, Lee Tracy and Shelley Berman.

VHS: S11434. $19.98.
Franklin J. Schaffner, 1964, 104 mins.

Best of the Fests 1990

An eclectic mixed-genre collection of award-winning short films. The program provides an entertaining, vigorous overview of 1990's most accomplished animation, comedy, documentary, dramatic and experimental films, including highly innovative gay and lesbian works. Of particular note are *Triangle*, an expressionist piece about the creation of the pink triangle, and *Song from an Angel*, which features Rodney Price as an AIDS patient. 90 mins.

VHS: S13833. $19.95.

The Best Way

Former Truffaut and Godard assistant Claude Miller made this acute social drama about an aggressively masculine athletic director of a boys' school who is attracted to a cross-dressing drama instructor. The athletic director's confused identity leads to a tense inner conflict over his long-suppressed sexuality. Also known as *The Best Way to Walk*. Cinematography by Bruno Nuytten. With Patrick Dewaere, Patrick Bouchitey and Christine Pascal. French with English subtitles.

VHS: S00120. $49.95.
Claude Miller, France, 1975, 85 mins.

The Best Man

The Best Man

Beyond Therapy

Robert Altman's off-center adaptation of Christopher Durang's play about the bizarre sexual and romantic entanglements of a group of New Yorkers. The central affair is a madcap encounter between bisexual Jeff Goldblum and prototypical nice girl Julie Hagarty. Altman weaves in a collection of eccentric weirdos, crazed mothers and pathologically freaked-out shrinks. The film "merges the romantic merry-go-round antics of *La Ronde* with the clamorous, overflowing narrative tactics of *Nashville*" (*Time Out*). With Glenda Jackson, Tom Conti, Christopher Guest and Genevieve Page.

VHS: S05215. $19.95.

Robert Altman, USA, 1987, 93 mins.

A Bigger Splash

An improvised, highly impressionistic look at the art, life and personal explorations of British painter David Hockney. The narrative is a loose collection of vignettes about love, art and sacrifice. The film is a candid and casual work loosely based on Hockney's break up with his lover, Peter Schlesinger. With Celia Birtwell, Mo McDermott and Henry Geldzahler.

VHS: S08116. $69.95.

Jack Hazan, Great Britain, 1974, 105 mins.

The Birdcage

Robin Williams and Nathan Lane star as the gay couple in this adaptation of the classic French farce *La Cage aux Folles*. They camp it up big to impress their son's prospective in-laws, played by Gene Hackman and Dianne Wiest. Of course, it all goes wrong but not before some big laughs emerge, and there is the rare opportunity to see Hackman in drag.

VHS: S29827. $19.98.

Mike Nichols, USA, 1996, 119 mins.

The Bitter Tears of Petra Von Kant

Film critic Molly Haskell described *The Bitter Tears of Petra Von Kant* as "a tragi-comic love story disguised as a lesbian slumber party in high-camp drag." Rainer Werner Fassbinder's highly stylized melodrama unfolds in the florid setting of an apartment dominated by fleshy nudes and cold, ivory mannequins. Three lesbians struggle for emotional control: a successful and "liberated" fashion designer; her contented and silent slave girl; and a sultry but cruel model who ends up making the master her slave. The dynamics of their interrelations are played out in this claustrophobic, self-contained world, set to the music of The Platters and Giuseppe Verdi. Cinematography by Michael Ballhaus. With Margit Carstensen, Hanna Schygulla, Irm Hermann and Katrin Schaake. German with English subtitles.

VHS: S13914. $79.95.

Rainer W. Fassbinder, W. Germany, 1972, 124 mins.

Black Lizard

A hilarious caper movie originally written for the stage by Yukio Mishima. The plot concerns a swanky female jewel thief who kidnaps nubile youths and ferries them to a hilariously glitzoid secret island. There she turns them into naked love statues—one of them bizarrely played by Mishima himself. Miss Lizard is portrayed by the silky transvestite actor Akihiro Miwa, who flounces around in an impossible collection of boas and chokers and turns every flourish of her cigarette holder into an over-the-top arabesque. Called "a tale of love, passion, greed and necrophilia" by *The New York Times*. Japanese with English subtitles.

VHS: S16261. $49.95.

Kinji Fukasaku, Japan, 1968, 90 mins.

Black Widow

Bob Rafelson's edgy, complicated police drama about a lonely, obsessive federal agent (Debra Winger) tracking a beautiful master criminal (Theresa Russell) who seduces, marries and kills wealthy men. Rafelson uses an ingenious set-up, crosscutting between their separate lives to establish the women's separate though shared identities. Rafelson burrows into the powerful sexual and emotional attraction between the two women. With Dennis Hopper, Sami Frey, Nicol Williamson, Mary Woronov and Terry O'Quinn. Cinematography by Conrad Hall. Score by Michael Small.

VHS: S04339. $19.98.

Bob Rafelson, USA, 1986, 103 mins.

Blind Trust

A gripping French-Canadian thriller in the vein of Stanley Kubrick's *The Killers*, about the cool planning, execution and bloody aftermath of an elaborate armored car robbery in Montreal. The homosexual guard taken prisoner fights back against his tormentors. With Marie Tifo, Pierre Curzi, Yvan Ponton and Jean-Louis Millette. English dubbed.

VHS: S05892. $79.98.

Yves Simoneau, Canada, 1986, 86 mins.

Blonde Death

Called "a warped cross between *Badlands* and the John Waters film of your choice" by *The L.A. Weekly*, James Dillinger's video boasts an original score by the Angry Samoans and a lurid plot-line involving two hypocritical, Bible-pounding suburbanites, the couple's rock-and-roll, sex-crazed blond nymphet daughter, her lesbian girlfriend, a jail-breaking boyfriend and the boyfriend's former prison lover. Dillinger wrote, directed, produced, photographed and edited this tongue-in-cheek melodrama.

VHS: S06256. Currently out of print. May be available for rental in some video stores.

James Dillinger, USA, 1987, 85 mins.

Blood and Roses

Roger Vadim's atmospheric adaptation of Sheridan Le Fanu's novel *Carmilla, Blood and Roses* is the lesbian vampire story of a jealous, uneasy young woman who is determined to trace her family's bizarre relationship with vampires. The woman's uncanny resemblance to her ancestor—a notorious vampire—creates an unsettling transference when she begins to adopt the vampire's tendencies and habits. Cinematography by Claude Renoir. Music by Jean Prodromides. With Mel Ferrer, Elsa Martinelli, Annette Vadim and Marc Allegret.

VHS: S16886. $19.95.

Roger Vadim, France/Italy, 1960, 87 mins.

Blood of a Poet

Jean Cocteau's first film is a work about the mysteries, dangers and rewards of an artist's life and work. The film has no recognizable narrative; it is constructed from a rush of images about a poet (played by photographer Lee Miller) caught in a dream-like trance, a magical mirror that allows him to view an artist (Enrique Rivero) suspended in time and trapped by the dimensions of his own work. "The movie has an

avant-garde roughness and unpredictability in its construction and use of symbols, but it's fundamentally…a study of the joys and agonies of being an artist" (*Time Out*). Cinematography by Georges Perinal. With Pauline Carton, Odette Talazac and Jean Desbordes. Minimal French dialog with no English subtitles.
VHS: S17880. $29.95.
Jean Cocteau, France, 1930, 54 mins.

Bloodhounds of Broadway

Howard Brookner (*Burroughs*) died before finishing this, his first feature. Set during the Roaring Twenties and based on four short stories by Damon Runyon, *Bloodhounds of Broadway* is a comic musical salute which stars Madonna as a nightclub singer, Rutger Hauer as a gangster and Matt Dillon as a gambler. The convoluted plot includes Madonna's confession that she wants to give up being a "jazz baby" and retire to Newark to raise babies and chickens. With Randy Quaid, Julie Hagerty and Josef Sommer.
VHS: S11574. $14.95.
Howard Brookner, USA, 1989, 93 mins.

BloodSisters

San Francisco's dyke leather community bears it all in this comprehensive documentary about the pleasures and pains of sadomasochism. Footage from key S/M leather competitions along with images from the 1993 March on Washington and the 25th Anniversary of Stonewall in New York are joined with insightful interviews. This film employs experimental and documentary styles as well as girl punk music.
VHS: S27615. $35.00.
Michelle Handelman, USA, 1995, 77 mins.

The Blue Hour

The third feature by Swiss-born Marcel Gisler tells about the odd affair between two Berliners: Theo, a hip young callboy, and Marie, his French neighbor, who recently split up with Paul. *The Blue Hour* is a lyrical, textured look at male prostitution and at gay men who sleep with women, at once sexy and probing. With Andreas Herder, Dina Leipzig, Cyrill Rey-Coquais. German with English subtitles.
VHS: S19446. $39.95.
Marcel Gisler, Germany, 1992, 87 mins.

Blue Jeans

An unsettling account of sexual identity and self-definition in which a young French boy travels to England and enjoys his first sexual experiences. When his girlfriend takes up with a more experienced lover, the despondent young man confides in his supervisor, who then ruthlessly exploits him for his own sexual gratification. French with English subtitles.
VHS: S00158. $59.95.
Hugues des Roziers, France, 1978, 80 mins.

Boys in Love

This collection of award-winning gay short films includes four worldwide festival favorites. *Death in Venice, CA* is the story of a repressed academic who is seduced by his landlady's stepson. The animated *Achilles*, by Academy Award-nominated animator Bary Purves, features Greek heroes and lovers Achilles and Petroclus as they battle the Trojans. *My Polish Waiter* focuses on a young man's infatuation with a silent, handsome waiter. In *Miguel, Ma Belle*, a recently spurned Latin man finds love again with the help of a dog. Together, the films form a bold look at love and sex in the '90s. 83 mins.
VHS: S28484. $29.95.

Boys in the Band

One of the first American films to openly deal with homosexuality, William Friedkin's *Boys in the Band* is adapted from Mort Crowley's play, and examines the bitter but camp experiences of gay life in a far less tolerant time, the 1960s. Using a birthday celebration as the launching point, the film juxtaposes two extremes, the closeted male and the exuberant queen. Set entirely in a New York apartment, the participants are eight openly gay men and one who refuses to come out of the closet. Originally controversial because of its bleak view, it helped inspire protests against director William Friedkin when he announced his later production *Cruising*, roughly ten years later. With Kenneth Nelson, Peter White, Leonard Frey and Cliff Gorman.
VHS: S00176. $59.98.
William Friedkin, USA, 1975, 119 mins.

The Boys of Cellblock Q

Director Alan Daniels adapts John C. Wall's off-Broadway play as a sly melodrama about the sexual and political corruption within a correction facility for young boys. The film is styled after 1930s

confused-young-man movies (such as *Fortune and Men's Eyes*). With Andrew Adams, Lewis Alante, Slade Burrus and Ken Merckx.
VHS: S18246. $29.95.
Alan Daniels, USA, 1992, 85 mins.

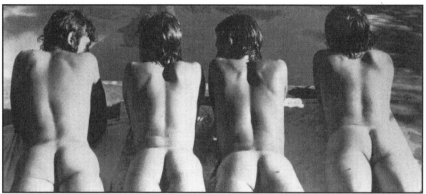

A Bigger Splash

The Boys of St. Vincent

Henry Czerny stars as a Brother Peter Lavin, the stern and difficult guardian of the boys of St. Vincent's Orphanage, who guards a terrible secret. He molests his favorite charges with near impunity until he is exposed by a janitor. A local policeman investigates and several of the abused boys come forward to tell their stories. Conspiring to save the reputation of the Catholic-run orphanage, the concerned authorities decide to keep Brother Lavin's actions hidden and bury the case. Fifteen years after this abuse comes to light, the victims refuse to remain silent and a new round of unsettling events develops. With Johnny Morina and Brian Dooley.
VHS: S27432. $89.95.
John N. Smith, Canada, 1994, 186 mins.

Brain Candy

The cast of *The Kids in the Hall*, the over-the-top Canadian comedy show, appeared together for the last time in this, their first feature film. A happiness drug threatens to consume the nation. This plot gives the Kids plenty of excuses to trot out their best characterization skills, especially their terrific drag. Bruce McCulloch, Kevin McDonald, Mark McKinney, and Scott Thompson star.
VHS: S29866. $98.99.
Kelly Makin, USA, 1996, 89 mins.

Broken Noses

Renowned photographer Bruce Weber's highly stylized depiction of the small Portland, Oregon, boxing club for boys run by Andy Minsker, a charismatic, former lightweight fighter. Like Weber's documentary on Chet Baker (*Let's Get Lost*), the film is an extended text on the meaning of the male body. Weber uses Minsker's highly troubled life to address issues of masculinity, sexuality, strength and desire. Remarkably unaffected, Minsker reveals both a boxer's machismo and a life of unrealized pain. With a sinuous jazz score by Chet Baker, Gerry Mulligan and Julie London.

VHS: S16462. $29.95.
Bruce Weber, USA, 1987, 75 mins.

Burroughs

An unconventional documentary about outlaw American writer and iconoclast William S. Burroughs (*Queer*, *Naked Lunch*). Burroughs' cut-and-paste approach to writing radically reshaped American literature in the '50s and anticipated the spontaneity and improvisation of the Beat Movement. The film examines Burroughs' art and work—his working methods, themes and preoccupations—bracketed against his frequently unsettling personal life, his strained relationship with his brother and the circumstances behind his wife's accidental death.

Burroughs

VHS: S00193. $39.95.
Howard Brookner, USA, 1984, 90 mins.

By Design

A heartfelt work about an exuberant lesbian fashion designer (Patty Duke Astin) whose determination to bear a child is met with social and personal resistance as she goes out to look for a substitute father. With Sara Botsford, Saul Rubinek and Sonia Zimmer. A strong personal drama from Claude Jutra, the director of the landmark Canadian feature *Mon Oncle Antoine*.

VHS: S00197. Currently out of print. May be available for rental in some video stores.
Claude Jutra, Canada, 1981, 88 mins.

Director **Pedro Almodovar** (b. 1951) was born in Calzada de Calatrava, an isolated village in southwestern Spain. Almodovar's early passions were music, literature and movies. When he was 17, he moved to Madrid. Unable to afford college, Almodovar did a number of odd jobs, while also contributing comic strips and articles for several underground publications, including *Star*, *Vibora* and *Vibraciones*. Almodovar supported himself by taking a job at the National Telephone Company, where he worked for 10 years.

In the '70s, Almodovar joined the prominent cutting edge theater group Los Golidardos, and appeared as an extra in several films. With no national film school for formal training, Almodovar was forced to teach himself the mechanics of filmmaking. He bought a Super-8 camera and began experimenting on short films with his friends and colleagues from the theater.

A new climate of artistic freedom emerged in the aftermath of Franco's death. Almodovar seized on these opportunities to write several short stories, a porno-photo novel (*All Yours*) and a novella (*Fire in the Guts*), and to create, in serial form, a popular character, "Patti Diphusa," who was an international porno star. Almodovar was also a regular contributor to a number of important publications, including *El Pais*, *Diario 16* and *La Luna*. In 1980, Almodovar directed his first feature, *Pepi, Luci, Bom and a Whole Lot of Other Girls*, about a woman who leaves her psychotic husband to have a lesbian affair. Almodovar financed the film, made for $10,000, by borrowing money from his friends.

During the early '80s, Almodovar also performed with the rock group Almodovar and McNamara. In 1982, he made his second film, *Labyrinth of Passion*. Early on, Almodovar developed a unique film aesthetic that combined a freewheeling mixture of styles that were informed by an outrageous camp sensibility. Almodovar is attracted to Madrid's hyperkinetic street life. His films feature deliberately stylized sets, expressive decor, and neon, soft colors, complemented by ludicrous plots and colorful casts. In describing his working methods, Almodovar recently said, "While I'm writing I design the set in my head. It's as if I were a painter. I begin by choosing a dominant theme, then cover that surface, then I apply another layer. It takes a lot of time—I can't take decisions right at the start because colors, volumes, objects and fabrics have their own lives."

Pedro Almodovar

Like Rainer Werner Fassbinder and Robert Altman, Almodovar developed a stock company of actors, which includes Julieta Serrano, Chus Lampreave, Angel de Andres Lopez, Kiti Manver and, more recently, Victoria Abril and Antonio Banderas. His principal on-screen collaborator throughout the '80s was the actress Carmen Maura, who served as Almodovar's surrogate, a conduit for his attitudes and approach to art, movies and popular culture.

With *Matador* (1986) and *Law of Desire* (1987), Almodovar's work took on a more distinctly gay sensibility. He began to earn recognition outside of Spain and, for the first time, his films were shown in American art-house theaters, where they soon attracted a loyal audience. Almodovar was the subject of a retrospective at the 1988 Toronto Festival of Festivals. *Women on the Verge of a Nervous Breakdown* (1988) was his commercial breakthrough and his most stylistically assured film. Four of his most recent films, *Tie Me Up, Tie Me Down!* (1990), *High Heels* (1991), *Kika* (1993) and *The Flower of My Secret* (1995), are black comedies centered on women characters with plenty of kinky plot twists.

Women on the Verge of a Nervous Breakdown

Cabaret

C

Bob Fosse's dark musical beautifully merges the political and personal. Set in 1930s Berlin, Liza Minnelli stars as an innocent American showgirl at the decadent Kit Kat Klub. She becomes involved in a sexual triangle between her aristocratic English lover (Michael York) and a homosexual German baron (Helmut Griem). The finest performance of *Cabaret* belongs to the cabaret's impresario (Joel Grey). "Film journals will feast for years on shots from this picture; as it rolled along, I saw page after illustrated page from a not-too-distant book called *The Cinema of Bob Fosse*" (Stanley Kauffman). Cinematography by Barry Unsworth. With Fritz Wepper and Marisa Berenson.

VHS: S01837. $19.98.
Laser: LD72168. $39.98.
Bob Fosse, USA, 1972, 128 mins.

Caligula

Penthouse publisher Bob Guccione's extravagant attempt to combine the art house porno film with an opulent costume epic is adapted from a Gore Vidal screenplay, which the author disowned. The film is a succession of sexual couplings, screen violence and depravity. *Caligula* has achieved cult status in some quarters, though not necessarily for the right reasons. With Peter O'Toole, Malcolm McDowell, John Gielgud and Teresa Ann Savoy. The film is available in two forms, a 160-minute unrated version and a heavily edited, 103-minute R version. English dubbed.

VHS: (unrated) S05788. $59.95.
Tinto Brass, Italy, 1982, 105 mins.

Can't Stop the Music

Six members of The Village People fall for Valerie Perrine in this disco musical which is full of gay in-jokes. The macho clone look of the 1970s is especially amusing when transferred from The Village People to Bruce Jenner and Steve Guttenberg. It's a must for anyone with an interest in musicals. The choreography to "Y.M.C.A." must be seen to be believed. With Tammy Grimes and June Havoc.

VHS: S20417. $14.98.
Nancy Walker, USA, 1980, 124 mins.

The Canterbury Tales

Chaucer's classic text is boldly reimagined in Pier Paolo Pasolini's visually spare, lyrical adaptation. The film is studded with grotesque ladies, unfaithful husbands and sexually ambivalent pages. The second part of Pasolini's amazing story-cycle trilogy, bracketing *The Decameron* and *Arabian Nights*. "Pasolini creates visual magic where other directors would never see beyond the banal, and the humor is as rich as ever" (*Time Out*). Music by Ennio Morricone. Cinematography by Tonino Delli Colli. With Pasolini, Hugh Griffith, Laura Betti and Tom Baker. In English.
VHS: S07821. $79.95.
Pier Paolo Pasolini, Italy, 1971, 109 mins.

Caravaggio

Derek Jarman's work about the Renaissance painter is an astonishing film about memory, time and the artistic process. Set in 1610, during the last gasps of the painter's (Nigel Terry) life, the film is a

fragmented, elliptical collection of images. Jarman builds an elaborate romantic triangle involving Caravaggio, his model Ranuccio Thomasoni (Sean Bean) and Lena (Tilda Swinton), Ranuccio's lover. Lena was the inspiration Caravaggio invoked for his portrait of Magdalene and other figurative pieces. With Robbie Coltrane.
VHS: S06024. $79.95.
Derek Jarman, Great Britain, 1986, 97 mins.

Caravaggio

Carrington

Emma Thompson gives a terrific performance as Dora Carrington, an unorthodox, androgynous painter from the early 20th century Bloomsbury Group, who passionately loves queer writer Giles Lytton-Strachey (Jonathan Pryce). The highly regarded playwright Christopher Hampton (*Les Liaisons Dangereuses*) directs this tight, witty and insightful period piece set amidst the self-conscious world of broken conventions and sexual eccentricities that come to mind whenever the name of the Bloomsbury Group is uttered.
VHS: S27596. $19.95.
Laser: LD75532. $34.95.
Christopher Hampton, Great Britain, 1995, 116 mins.

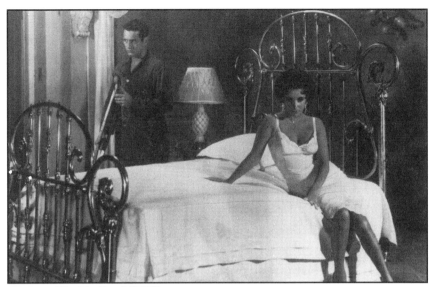
Cat on a Hot Tin Roof (1958)

Cass

A harrowing work about a disenchanted Australian filmmaker (Michelle Fawden) who is upset by the critical reaction to her film about a primitive culture. She becomes increasingly frustrated and unable to adjust to her "normal" life; the resultant cultural dislocation eventually destroys her marriage. She returns home to sort out her pain and is drawn to alternative lifestyles, ultimately entering into a casual affair with a vibrant young woman (Judy Morris). With John Waters and Peter Carroll.

VHS: S08147. Currently out of print. May be available for rental in some video stores.

Chris Noonan, Australia, 1978, 90 mins.

Cat on a Hot Tin Roof (1958)

An operatic adaptation of Tennessee Williams' play centered around themes of sexual ambivalence, greed and impotence in a wealthy Southern family. Paul Newman is confused by his sexuality; Elizabeth Taylor plays his neurotically unbalanced wife; and Burl Ives is the powerful, ruthless patriarch, who is slowly dying of cancer. The dramatic conflict is shaped by the intense internecine warfare set off when the heirs battle for control of the estate. With Judith Anderson, Jack Carson and Madeleine Sherwood.

VHS: S13776. $19.98.

Richard Brooks, USA, 1958, 108 mins.

Cat on a Hot Tin Roof (1984)

The Broadway revival of Tennessee Williams' Southern melodrama about sexual dysfunction and family strife in a decaying Southern aristocracy. Jessica Lange plays Maggie, the neurotic wife of the sexually ambivalent Brick (Tommy Lee Jones). Rip Torn is the cancer-ravaged, paternal Big Daddy. Made for American Playhouse television.

VHS: S07130. Currently out of print. May be available for rental in some video stores.
Laser: LD70541. $34.98.
Jack Hofsiss, USA, 1984, 122 mins.

Celeste

Celeste Albaret was Proust's housekeeper and confidante during the final nine years of his life. Percy Adlon's brave, ironic film details their subtle relationship. A work of delicacy and insight, adapted from Celeste's journals, the "film is a subtle, humorous and touching study of the loyal relationship between a middle-aged homosexual intellectual and a simple, caring girl" (*The Faber Companion to Foreign Films*). Cinematography by Jurgen Martin. With Eva Mattes, Jurgen Arndt, Norbert Wartha, Wolf Euba and Joseph Manoth. German and French with English subtitles.

VHS: S13915. $79.95.
Percy Adlon, W. Germany, 1981, 106 mins.

Celluloid Closet

Lily Tomlin, Shirley MacLaine, Tony Curtis, Susan Sarandon, Tom Hanks, Whoopi Goldberg and others provide the commentary to entertaining clips from over 120 films as we learn all the secrets and hear all the stories in this compilation of the history of homosexuality in Hollywood movies. A fun romp with some amazing pre-Breen-code early footage. "An indispensable addition to the history of Hollywood, with the popular appeal of *That's Entertainment*" (Janet Maslin, *New York Times*).

VHS: S30403. $97.99
Laser: LD76027. $39.95.
Rob Epstein/Jeffrey Friedman, USA, 1996, 102 mins.

Chanel Solitaire

An insightful biography of designer Coco Chanel (Marie-France Pisier) that documents her transformation from disadvantaged orphan to

breakthrough fashion designer. The movie looks at her colorful and provocative love life, including her lesbian affair with Misia Cert. With Timothy Dalton, Rutger Hauer, Karen Black and Brigitte Fossey.
VHS: S01509. $19.99.
George Kaczender, USA/France, 1981, 120 mins.

The Changer: A Record of the Times
Rare archival footage traces the rich musical history of the woman-centered record label Olivia Records. Music, concert footage, and interviews with Meg Christian, Holly Near, Margie Adam, June Millington, Vicki Randal and Bonnie Raitt reveal the legacy of the women's music movement.
VHS: S19450. $39.95.
Frances Reid/Judy Dlugacz, USA, 78 mins.

The Children's Hour
Based on a play by Lillian Hellman, and previously made into a film by Wyler in 1936 as *These Three*, this later film curiously compromises the overt lesbian subject matter of the original. Set in an exclusive girls' boarding school, the film stars Audrey Hepburn and Shirley MacLaine as two teachers who discipline a vindictive little girl. The child twists an overheard comment into slander and accuses the two of lesbianism; outraged, Hepburn and MacLaine fight back in court. With James Garner, Miriam Hopkins and Fay Bainter.
VHS: S13345. $19.98.
William Wyler, USA, 1961, 108 mins.

Chinese Roulette
This Brechtian satire centers around a young paraplegic (Andrea Schober) who orchestrates a rendezvous between her parents (Ulli Lommel and Margit Carstensen) and their respective lovers (Anna Karina and Volker Spengler) in an isolated country house. The young woman insists they play "Chinese Roulette," a truth-telling game that reveals shocking family secrets and long-standing resentments. One of Rainer Werner Fassbinder's most expressive films, *Chinese Roulette* emphasizes artifice over reality. Cinematography by Michael Ballhaus. German with English subtitles.
VHS: S12821. $29.95.
Rainer W. Fassbinder, W. Germany, 1976, 96 mins.

A Chorus Line

Richard Attenborough adapts Michael Bennett's landmark musical about a group of dancers and actors auditioning for a Broadway musical. The numbers range from the kinetic "I Hope I Get It" and comic "Dance Ten, Looks Three" to the mournful "At the Ballet" and cathartic "What I Did for Love." The play's humanism emerges from the individual stories, such as that of Cassie, the director's former lover who demands one last chance, and Paul, a tortured young man who talks about the difficulty of acknowledging his homosexuality. With Terrence Mann, Alyson Reed, Cameron English, Vicki Frederick and Janet Jones.

VHS: S02716. Currently out of print. May be available for rental in some video stores.

Sir Richard Attenborough, USA, 1985, 113 mins.

Citizen Cohn

A complex, powerful, made-for-cable biography of lawyer and conservative activist Roy Cohn, energetically played by James Woods. Adapted from Nicholas von Hoffman's biography, the film details Cohn's ruthless ambition and lust for power, his closeted homosexuality and his death from AIDS. In the hospital, he's visited by the ghosts of his past: his prosecution of the Rosenbergs, the Communist witch hunts in conjunction with Joseph McCarthy, his political battles with the Kennedys and the attempted destabilization of the civil rights movement. With Joe Don Baker, Joseph Bologna, Ed Flanders and Frederick Forrest.

VHS: S18790. $19.98.

Frank Pierson, USA, 1992, 112 mins.

Claire of the Moon

Nicole Conn's sensual, exploratory work concerns the shifting relationship of two women. Claire Jobrowski is the confused, promiscuous, heterosexual writer of romance novels. Dr. Noel Benedict is trying to recover from a disastrous love affair. The two are brought together at a writer's workshop in the Pacific Northwest. Initially at odds, Claire and Noel come to admit their attraction to each other through encounter sessions with their openly lesbian and outrageous host, Maggie. "An encouraging debut film about love between adults" (*L.A. Weekly*). Cinematography by Randolph Sellars. With Trisha Todd, Karen Trumbo, Faith McDevitt and Caren Graham.

VHS: S19102. $29.98.

Nicole Conn, USA, 1992, 102 mins.

The Children's Hour   *The Children's Hour*

The Clinic

In this quirky Australian social satire, Chris Haywood (*Breaker Morant*) plays an extroverted gay doctor working in a V.D. clinic. "From the doctors having marital problems and hangovers to the patients— gay, straight, first-timers, bizarre and just plain folk—*The Clinic* is a stage where everyone meets under stressful, vulnerable and embarassing circumstances and begins to heal with laughter, the most powerful medicine doled out" (Los Angeles Film Exposition). With Simon Burke, Rona McLeod and Gerda Nicolson.

VHS: S00249. Currently out of print. May be available for rental in some video stores.

David Stevens, Australia, 1985, 92 mins.

Club des Femmes

A pioneering feminist work that's a spirited critique of "the bastions of male supremacy," revolving around the activities and events of an all-girl hotel where men are barred. Danielle Darrieux is the nightclub performer whose intertwining fate with the other women is the source of mystery and tension. With Elsa Argal, Betty Stockfield and Eve Francis. French with English subtitles.

VHS: S00254. $34.95.

Jacques Deval, France, 1936, 90 mins.

A Cold Coming

A terse, well-acted adaptation of Howard Castle's play about erotic obsession, emotional depravity and sexual ruin, in which two lovers, Dave (Shawn Michael Kosel) and John (David Gadberry), attempt to tear down the various facades that impede their relationship. 70 mins.

VHS: S17372. Currently out of print. May be available for rental in some video stores.

Howard Casner, USA, 1992, 70 mins.

Colegas

Eloy de la Iglesia's sensitive though hard-edged portrait of the interlocking fates among working-class friends in Madrid. Jose and Antonio are two jobless youths and lovers, spending their days hanging around video arcades, getting high, hoping that something will change. The idyll is shattered when Jose impregnates Antonio's sister Rosario. With few alternatives, the three make the difficult trek to Morocco in order for Rosario to obtain an abortion. They are caught in a sinister web of drug smugglers and violent criminals in the seedy back alleys. "De la Iglesia's deep affection for youth, and the latent eroticism of friendship, glows from every frame" (*L.A. Style*). Spanish with English subtitles.

VHS: S01562. $89.95.
Eloy de la Iglesia, Spain, 117 mins.

Colonel Redl

The second part of Istvan Szabo's trilogy on power and ambition. Alfred Redl (Klaus Maria Brandauer), an ambitious, working-class military officer, conceals his homosexuality and sordid past and rises through the military ranks. He is eventually elevated to the position of head of military intelligence of the Austro-Hungarian empire. In this new position, he naturally makes enemies, and is framed by Archduke Franz Ferdinand for revealing state secrets to the Russians. "The director...never loses sight of his central concern—the ambiguity of Redl's nature and the ease with which he tells the lies that destroy him" (*The Faber Companion to Foreign Films*). Cinematography by Lajos Koltai. With Hans-Christian Blech, Armin Mueller-Stahl, Gudrun Landgrebe and Jan Niklas. Hungarian with English subtitles.

VHS: S03469. Currently out of print. May be available for rental in some video stores.
Laser: LD70923. Currently out of print. May be available for rental in some video stores.
Istvan Szabo, W. Germany/Hungary/Austria, 1984, 149 mins.

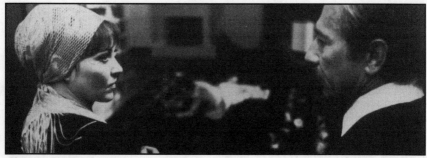

Chinese Roulette

The Color of Pomegranates (Director's Cut)

Sergei Paradjanov's greatest film is a ravishing and exotic mosaic on the life, art and the spiritual odyssey of the 18th-century Armenian poet Sayat Nova. The film is a mesmerizing collection of poetic images and beautifully arranged tableaux, interweaving landscapes, villages, costumes, props and gestures. Paradjanov's original version was taken out of his control and restructured under the supervision of Sergei Yutkevich. This director's cut repositions some of the shots and images and restores the censored footage. Paradjanov weaves "a sort of visionary parasurrealism through the most economical means of gesture, props and texture.... A sublime and heartbreaking film" (J. Hoberman, *Village Voice*). Cinematography by Suren and M. Shakhbazian. With Sofico Chiaureli, M. Aleksanian and V. Galstian. Armenian with English subtitles.

VHS: S19064. $29.95.
Sergei Paradjanov, USSR, 1969, 75 mins.

The Color Purple

Steven Spielberg's adaptation of Alice Walker's novel about growing up "poor, female, ugly and black" in the Deep South is a moving portrait of Celie's struggle for self-respect and freedom. Spielberg treads carefully around the novel's more radical homoerotic sub-plot, though Celie and blues singer Shug (Margaret Avery), do manage to have a lesbian love affair. With a powerful performance from Whoopi Goldberg. With Oprah Winfrey, Willard Pugh, Danny Glover and Rae Dawn Chong.

VHS: S03551. $19.98.
Laser: CAV version: LD70545. $59.98.
Laser: CLV version: LD70546. $29.98.
Steven Spielberg, USA, 1985, 154 mins.

Come Back to the Five and Dime, Jimmy Dean, Jimmy Dean

Robert Altman's adaptation of Ed Graczyk's play about a group of friends who gather for the 20-year reunion of a James Dean fan club. Altman uses the casual structure to show their hidden secrets and private failures. Sandy Dennis plays an ethereal, unbalanced woman who believes Dean is the father of her child. Karen Black plays a mysterious figure, a transsexual who hovers over the proceedings. With Cher, Susie Bond, Kathy Bates and Martha Heflin.

VHS: S00259. Currently out of print. May be available for rental in some video stores.
Robert Altman, USA, 1982, 110 mins.

Common Threads: Stories from the Quilt

Robert Epstein and Jeffrey Friedman's award-winning, compassionate documentary recreates the story behind five panels in the NAMES Quilt project. Each panel is devoted to someone who died of AIDS. The directors brilliantly evoke the stories of each individual through the memories of their family and friends. Included are: Dr. Tom Waddell, a one-time Olympic champion and co-founder of the Gay Games; a retired Navy commander who remembers his lover, a landscape architect; an 11-year-old hemophiliac remembered by his parents; Vito Russo, the writer, film critic and gay activist who describes his deceased lover Jeff Sevcik; and an IV drug user, recalled by his family. The film has an uninflected shape and quietly affirming depth. Narrated by Dustin Hoffman.

VHS: S12767. $19.98.
Robert Epstein/Jeffrey Friedman, USA, 1989, 79 mins.

The Conformist

Director Bernardo Bertolucci equates the rise of Italian fascism with the troubled psychosexual life of his protagonist, Marcello (Jean-Louis Trintignant). Marcello's conformity is rooted in his palpable need to expunge a homosexual incident from his youth—a molestation by an older man. "Bertolucci conjures a dazzling historical and personal perspective, demonstrating how the search for normality ends in the inevitable discovery that there is no such thing" (*Time Out*). With Stefania Sandrelli, Gastone Moschin, Enzo Taroscio, Pierre Clementi and Dominique Sanda. Cinematography by Vittorio Storaro. English dubbed.

VHS: S00264. Currently out of print. May be available for rental in some video stores.
Bernardo Bertolucci, Italy, 1970, 108 mins.

Consenting Adult

An intelligent adaptation of Laura Z. Hobson's novel that captures the violent emotions and conflicted family dynamics when a son (Barry Tubb) admits to his shocked parents that he's gay. The narrative explores the father's (Martin Sheen) subsequent withdrawal into denial and estrangement, and the mother's (Marlo Thomas) efforts to heal the wounds and save the family. With Talia Balsam, Ben Piazza and Corrine Michaels.

VHS: S09046. Currently out of print. May be available for rental in some video stores.
Gilbert Cates, USA, 1982, 100 mins.

Conversation Piece

An idiosyncratic late period work from Luchino Visconti that was completed following a long illness. Burt Lancaster is a repressed homosexual and iconoclastic professor who insists on an orderly, refined life at his opulent 18th-century Rome apartment. His solitary existence is shattered by the appearance of a wealthy countess (Silvana Mangano), her daughter (Claudia Marsani) and her sexually ambivalent friends, including a revolutionary student leader (Helmut Berger). Cinematography by Pasqualino De Santis. With Claudia Cardinale.

VHS: S00268. $29.95.
Luchino Visconti, Italy/France, 1975, 121 mins.

Coup de Grace

Volker Schlondorff's somber, understated adaptation of Marguerite Yourcenar's novel about the contradictory feelings and buried passions of an ambivalent sex triangle. Set after the First World War, the film deals with the interlocking obsessions of a German officer (Matthias Habich) assigned to fight Communist insurgents in the Baltic region. He rejects a beautiful, troubled Nazi sympathizer (filmmaker Margarethe von Trotta) and seduces her ascetic brother (Rudiger Kirschstein). Cinematography by Igor Luther. With Matthieu Carriere and Valeska Gert. German with English subtitles.

VHS: S00274. Currently out of print. May be available for rental in some video stores.
Volker Schlondorff, W. Germany, 1976, 95 mins.

Cruising

A Hollywood-produced crime thriller set in New York's gay world, *Cruising* features Al Pacino as a cop who goes underground to capture a bloody killer whose victims are all homosexuals. William Friedkin (*The French Connection*) directed a cast that includes Paul Sorvino, Karen Allen, Richard Cox and Don Scardino, and shot the film in gritty, "realistic" locations. But the false and ugly representation of the gay world as "sick" led to a storm of national protest against the film when it was theatrically released.

VHS: S19447. $19.98.
William Friedkin, USA, 1980, 106 mins.

The Crying Game

Irish filmmaker Neil Jordan's moody and intricate film about erotic obsession and romantic pessimism charts a fractured world of deception, abandon and terror. Stephen Rea is a reluctant IRA terrorist who participates in the abduction of a black British soldier (Forest Whitaker). In exile, Rea ends up protecting a beautiful, mysterious London chanteuse connected to the soldier's past. *The Crying Game* is a daring meditation on politics, sex, class and race. With Miranda Richardson and the amazing Jaye Davidson. Music by Anne Dudley. Cinematography by Ian Wilson. Academy Award for Best Original Screenplay.

VHS: S18749. $19.98.
Neil Jordan, Great Britain, 1992, 112 mins.

Curse of the Queerwolf

Lawrence Smalbut and Richard Cheese are just average macho guys who court disaster when they pick up two mysterious women. Just as Smalbut realizes that his date is no lady, she/he bites him on the derriere and forever transforms his life. Now when the moon is full, Smalbut finds himself magically transformed into "Queerwolf," a drag queen werewolf. It's a campy horror romp in questionable taste.

VHS: S27659. $14.95.
Mark Pirro, USA, 1994, 90 mins.

Cynara

Described by its maker as "a lesbian *Wuthering Heights*," this video brings the homoerotic tensions inherent in many gothic works into view. Johanna Nemeth and Melissa Nazila star as the sexy and attractive lovers. From the director of *Claire of the Moon*.

VHS: S29784. $29.95.
Nicole Conn, USA, 1996, 35 mins.

Cynara

The Damned

D

Luchino Visconti's operatic allegory about the rise of German fascism centers on the diabolical dynamics of the Essenbecks, a family of powerful weapons manufacturers. The film explores the collaboration between the Nazi hierarchy and Germany's ruling class. *The Damned* also exposes the decadence of the family; in a great scene, Helmut Berger—outfitted in Dietrich drag—is humiliated by Nazi officials. Cinematography by Armando Nannuzzi and Pasquale De Santis. Music by Maurice Jarre. With Dirk Bogarde, Ingrid Thulin, Renaud Verley, Helmut Griem and Charlotte Rampling. English dubbed.

VHS: S00293. $59.95.
Luchino Visconti, Italy/W. Germany, 1969, 164 mins.

Dark Habits

Pedro Almodovar's third feature is a sacrilegious black comedy set in a decaying Madrid convent that is ruled by a drug-addicted Mother Superior with a voracious sexual appetite. The narrative is shaken up by the appearance of a campy nightclub performer, who insinuates herself into the convent and unleashes her own peculiar habits. "Hilarious, irreverent fun. Part Luis Bunuel, part John Waters camp. Lots of laughs" (*The Village Voice*). Cinematography by Angel L. Fernandez. With Cristina Pascual, Julieta Serrano, Marisa Paredes and Carmen Maura. Spanish with English subtitles.

VHS: S08103. $79.95.
Pedro Almodovar, Spain, 1984, 116 mins.

Darling

Julie Christie plays a London commoner whose androgynous features propel her into a modeling superstar. But she conceals her boredom and disenchantment with her marriage to a wealthy Italian prince, aimlessly pursues a romance with journalist Dirk Bogarde, and then floats into an affair with Laurence Harvey. Her photographer friend (Roland Curram) alternately sleeps with her and with an Italian waiter. Christie won the Best Actress Academy Award for her portrayal of the pretty, spoiled model.

VHS: S00305. Currently out of print. May be available for rental in some video stores.
Laser: LD70358. $69.95.
John Schlesinger, Great Britain, 1965, 127 mins.

Daughters of Darkness

On their honeymoon, a socially awkward couple become unwitting pawns in the calculating intrigue of Elisabeth Bathory (Delphine Seyrig), a lesbian vampire. The story unfolds in a deserted hotel on the Belgian coast where several missing children are found, their bodies drained of blood. "Kumel brings the myth's kinkier aspects to the fore in their full glory. Gorgeous, absolutely bloody gorgeous" (*Time Out*). With Daniele Ouimet, John Karlen, Andrea Rau and Paul Esser. French with English subtitles.

VHS: S00306. Currently out of print. May be available for rental in some video stores.
Harry Kumel, France/Belgium/W. Germany/Italy, 1971, 96 mins.

Daughters of the Dust

This remarkable first feature by Julie Dash explores the family dynamics and sexual tensions of three generations of African-American women at the turn of the century. Structured around the family's migration from the Sea Island to the mainland, the film focuses on the return of the family pariah, Yellow Mary (Barbara-O), accompanied by her beautiful and mysterious female companion. The film is told through a highly unusual narrative device, related by an unborn child. With Cora Lee Day, Alva Rogers, Turla Hoosier and Kaycee Moore.

VHS: S16913. $24.95.
Julie Dash, USA, 1991, 113 mins.

David Hockney: Portrait of an Artist

A portrait of the gay artist and designer David Hockney. In this fascinating, no-holds-barred account, Hockney allowed the documentary crew unprecedented access to his London studio. The result is an intimate look at his methodology and peculiar work habits. 55 mins.

VHS: S01624. $39.95.
Don Featherstone, Great Britain, 1983, 55 mins.

David Hockney at the Tate

Since he emerged on the London art scene in the mid-60s, David Hockney has become one of the most distinctive British painters in avant-garde and commercial circles. On the occasion of the artist's 50th birthday, London's Tate Gallery staged a major retrospective of his work. Melvyn Bragg appears with Hockney at the gallery for a personal appraisal of the exhibition, as the two discuss Hockney's diverse career. 55 mins.

VHS: S10266. $39.95.
Laser: LD70115. $39.95.

Allen Benson, Great Britain, 1983, 55 mins.

The Dear Boys

A groundbreaking work adapted from Gerard Reve's novel about the romantic and sexual entanglements of a morose, self-absorbed writer. He is fearful that aging will rob him of youthful companionship and so, together with his manipulative young sex partner, he plots to seduce a gentle young man from the arms of an older lover. With Hugo Metsers, Hans Dagelet, Bill Van Dijk and Albert Moi. Dutch with English subtitles.

VHS: S17444. $69.95.

Paul de Lussanet, Holland, 1980, 90 mins.

Death in Venice

Luchino Visconti's film is a sumptuous, operatic adaptation of Thomas Mann's novella. It is a meditation on beauty; its powerful themes are erotic obsession and unconsummated desire. The protagonist Aschenbach (Dirk Bogarde) is a composer who visits Venice to reinvigorate his imagination. Instead he becomes infatuated with the beauty, youth and incorruptibility of a young Polish boy (Bjorn Andresen). Cinematography by Pasquale De Santis. Brilliant use of Gustav Mahler's music. With Silvana Mangano and Marisa Berenson. English dubbed.

VHS: S00316. $59.95.

Luchino Visconti, Italy, 1970, 130 mins.

David Hockney: Portrait of an Artist

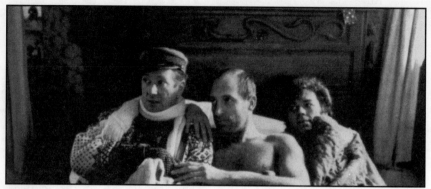
The Dear Boys

Decameron

The first part of Pier Paolo Pasolini's trilogy (followed by *The Canterbury Tales* and *Arabian Nights*) is adapted from eight Boccaccio tales. Pasolini created a vibrant mosaic linking mischievous nuns, three insanely jealous brothers, a false prophet and various tales of sexual intrigue and lust. Pasolini himself appears in one of the vignettes, as the painter Giotto. Cinematography by Tonino Delli Colli. Music by Ennio Morricone. With Franco Citti, Ninetto Davoli, Angeli Luce and Patrizia Capparelli. Italian with English subtitles.
VHS: S08260. $79.95.
Pier Paolo Pasolini, Italy, 1970, 111 mins.

Der Sprinter

A spirited comedy about a sexually ambivalent young man whose parents are distressed by his homosexual inclinations. In a bid for conformity and acceptance, he takes up track and field and promptly falls for a female shot putter. With Wieland Samolak. German with English subtitles.
VHS: S02187. $59.95.
Christopher Boll, W. Germany, 1983, 90 mins.

Desert Hearts

A sympathetic, perceptive lesbian drama set in the late 1950s about a repressed New York literature professor (Helen Shaver) who arrives in Reno for a quick divorce and succumbs to the aggressive tactics of a beautiful, free-spirited sculptress (the amazing Patricia Charbonneau), who lives on a dude ranch. The film is notable for its ensemble acting, director Donna Deitch's casual, uninflected visual style and the characters' expressive, complicated emotional range. Adapted from

Janice Rule's novel *Desert of the Heart*. With Audra Lindley, Andra Akers, Dean Butler and Alex McArthur.

VHS: S01919. $19.98.

Donna Deitch, USA, 1985, 96 mins.

Desire

Director Stuart Marshall chronicles the events leading to a crucial chapter in the gay and lesbian movement's history: the imprisonment of homosexuals in Nazi concentration camps during World War II. His film examines the "discovery" of homosexuality by the medical and psychoanalytic professions in the 1890s, and the subsequent movements in Germany during the early years of this century demanding recognition of gay and lesbian rights.

VHS: S16632. $39.95.

Stuart Marshall, Great Britain, 1989, 88 mins.

Despair

Rainer Werner Fassbinder's chilling, English-language translation of Vladimir Nabokov's novel about Hermann Hermann (Dirk Bogarde), who devises a curious plot to murder another man and then pass him off as himself, so as to collect the insurance money. Fassbinder uses language, comic disorder, body movements and gesture to convey a sinister, disquieting air of intrigue. "Exceptionally daring and clever...an insanely brilliant conspiracy of talent" (Roger Ebert, *Chicago Sun-Times*). Screenplay adaptation by English playwright Tom Stoppard. With Andrea Ferreol, Volker Spengler, Klaus Lowitsch and Alexander Allerson.

VHS: S00323. Currently out of print. May be available for rental in some video stores.

Rainer W. Fassbinder, W. Germany/France, 1977, 119 mins.

Desperate Living

An outlandish film from John Waters shot in a fragmented, hyper absurd comic style, the story concerns a woman (Mink Stole)—just released from a mental asylum—who believes her family is trying to kill her. With the help of her overweight maid, she murders her husband and seeks refuge in a freakish community populated by killers, transsexuals and the horribly disfigured. With Liz Renay, Susan Lowe and Edith Massey.

VHS: S00324. $19.98.

John Waters, USA, 1977, 90 mins.

The Devils

Ken Russell's outrageous, frequently scorned, sacrilegious shocker is freely adapted from John Whiting's play and the Aldous Huxley novel *The Devils of Loudon*. The sensational story concerns a 17th-century witchhunt authorities undertake to destroy a group of French nuns they believe are demonically possessed. *The Devils*' campy, deadpan wit finds a perfect corollary in Russell's depiction of masturbating nuns and tortured priests. Derek Jarman designed the sets. Cinematography by David Watkin. With Vanessa Redgrave, Oliver Reed, Dudley Sutton and Max Adrian.

VHS: S00334. $19.98.
Ken Russell, Great Britain, 1971, 105 mins.

The Devil's Playground

Fred Schepisi's autobiographical feature debut is set in a rigid Catholic boarding school of the 1950s. The film contrasts the fortunes of several young men confronting the pain and confusion of their underdeveloped sexual identities. "A comedy of sympathy about the old Christian fear of sex. *The Devil's Playground* drips with desire, and it is quietly funny without any mockery" (David Elliott). Cinematography by Ian Baker. With Arthur Dignam, Nick Tate, Simon Burke and Charles McCallum.

VHS: S03615. Currently out of print. May be available for rental in some video stores.
Fred Schepisi, Australia, 1978, 105 mins.

Discovery Program, Short Stories

Four shorts make up this compelling collection, highlighted by the Academy Award-winning *Ray's Male Heterosexual Dance Hall*, with David Rasche and Fred Willard; *Hearts of Stone*; *The Open Window* and *Greasy Lake*, which was adapted from T. Corraghessan Boyle's acclaimed short story about rites of passage. With Eric Stoltz, James Spader and Tegan West.

VHS: S14010. Currently out of print. May be available for rental in some video stores.

Dominique in "Daughters of Lesbos"

Oversexed women bare it all as they pursue sapphic pleasures in a hothouse of emotion. Their club, known as the New York City Man Haters Society, is not a group with which to trifle. One outrageous peeping tom learns this lesson when he seduces a lesbian by slipping her a mickey. He quickly finds out that a lesbian's vengeance can be swift like a knife. With Claudia Cheer, Jo Sweet, Sue Akers and Carla Costa.

VHS: S27675. $19.98.

Peter Woodcock, USA, 1967, 65 mins.

Dona Herlinda and Her Son

A provocative gay farrago about deception and concealment. A young doctor carries on a passionate affair with a student, but their liaisons are hampered by a lack of privacy. This is resolved when the student moves in with the doctor and his mother, Dona Herlinda. Though this makes life easier, the doctor marries a beautiful woman to satisfy his demanding mother. A daring critique of Latin machismo, director Jaime Humberto Hermosillo presents a dark, amusing portrait of social and sexual conformity. "Sly, deadpan comedy. The ultimate gay homage to mom" (David Denby, New York). With Arturo Meza, Marco Antonio Trevino, Leticia Lupersio and Guadalupe Del Toro. Spanish with English subtitles.

VHS: S06022. $79.95.

Jaime H. Hermosillo, Mexico, 1986, 90 mins.

Dorian Gray

Helmut Berger (*The Damned*) stars as the title character in this adaptation of Oscar Wilde's novel. Shifted to the present, the story charts the disaffection and sexually forbidden exploits of an impossibly vain, idle young man who never ages. With Richard Todd, Herbert Lom, Marie Liljedahl and Beryl Cunningham.

VHS: S04258. $14.98.

Massimo Dallamano, Italy/W. Germany/Lichtenstein, 1970, 92 mins.

Desperate Living

Drawing the Line: A Portrait of Keith Haring

A wonderful portrait of the late Keith Haring, the film traces his career from an anonymous graffiti artist who drew chalk figures on New York City subway posters to being called the successor to Andy Warhol and Roy Lichtenstein. Includes interviews with gallery owners Leo Castelli and Tony Shafrazi and actor/friend/collector Dennis Hopper.
VHS: S12594. $19.95.
Elisabeth Aubert, USA, 1989, 30 mins.

Dream Boys Revue

Ruth Buzzi and Lyle Waggoner are the bizarre hosts of this talent and beauty contest in which the beautiful "women" are, in fact, all men. In this extravagant camp competition held in Texas, female impersonators of Ann-Margret, Liza Minnelli, Bette Davis, Marilyn Monroe and Barbra Streisand compete for stardom.
VHS: S03950. $19.95.
Howard Schwartz/John Moriarty, USA, 1985, 74 mins.

Dream Man

An adaptation of James Carroll Pickett's one-man theater performance stars Michael Kearns as a Lenny Bruce-like commentator who conjures up elaborate, witty and profane sexual fantasies over the phone lines. "Straight-forward, poetically insightful," wrote *Daily Variety*. Written and directed by Hugh Harrison (*Jerker*). Music by Craig Lee. With an introduction by controversial performance artist Tim Anderson and an interview with the playwright. From the Pride Playhouse series.
VHS: S17117. $19.95.
Hugh Harrison, USA, 1991, 90 mins.

The Dresser

Peter Yates adapts Ronald Harwood's witty, dark play about the precarious relationship of the domineering touring company actor and manager (Albert Finney) and his submissive, effeminate dresser (Tom Courtenay) as they travel through the war-torn English countryside with their production of *King Lear*. Yates evokes a specific time and place and shapes highly distinctive performances from his actors. With Edward Fox, Zena Walker, Eileen Atkins and Michael Gough.
VHS: S00374. $14.95.
Peter Yates, Great Britain, 1983, 118 mins.

Dominique in "Daughters of Lesbos"

Drifting

Reportedly the first gay film made in Israel, Amos Guttman's controversial feature debut captures the pain and frustration of an isolated, distraught filmmaker haunted by artistic failure and a growing sense of impotence and mediocrity. He rejects his friends and lover and retreats into a hermetically sealed, self-destructive world. "The best gay film ever made!" (*New York Native*). With Jonathan Seagalle. Hebrew with English subtitles.

VHS: S00376. $69.95.

Amos Guttman, Israel, 1982, 80 mins.

Drugstore Cowboy

Portland independent Gus Van Sant's savagely comic essay stars Matt Dillon as the forlorn leader of a criminal gang that robs pharmaceutical stores. Van Sant has a keen eye for the poetry and ragged, casual rootlessness of the streets. The film is a stark and unsentimental portrait of what William S. Burroughs identified as the "algebra of need." Adapted from an unpublished novel by James Boggle. Wonderful supporting performances from Kelly Lynch, James Le Gros, Heather Graham, James Remar and Burroughs as Father Tom, a defrocked junkie priest.

VHS: S11724. $14.98.
Laser: LD70955. $39.95.

Gus Van Sant, USA, 1989, 100 mins.

Director **Gregg Araki** (b. 1963) stands out among a new generation of queer filmmakers for his bleak view of teens and young adults in contemporary life. From his very first film, *Three Bewildered People* (1987), he has dealt with the aimlessness and angst that seems to characterize the generation of the late 1980s and the early 1990s. This film set a pattern for stylishly realized stories, tinged with despair, and produced on a low budget that would only change, at least in terms of finances, with *The Doom Generation* (1995). Also characteristic of Araki's work is a continuing interest in the evolving

sexual awareness of youth. His characters, even when openly gay, often eschew the trappings of older, more established lesbian and gay lifestyles and inhabit a more sexually ambiguous world.

The Long Weekend of Despair (1989) joins a group of lesbian, gay, and straight friends who reminisce about college before seguing into a mix of angst and sexual play. Araki's open disregard for the dictates of critics and community spokespeople has often earned him heated criticism. In *The Living End* (1992), two sexy, HIV-positive, gay men set off for a road movie of gratuitous violence, sex and revilement. This unflattering view of the AIDS epidemic was widely criticized, though many loved its style and open dependence on earlier works by Godard, Warhol and John Waters. *Totally F***ed Up* (1994) tackles the problems of disoriented teens coming to terms with being queer and other problems associated with growing up. The film mixes narrative and mock interviews to tell the story of a group of Los Angeles teens but ultimately comes to focus on one particularly photogenic, gay young man. In this film, as happens so often in Araki's earlier work, gay love comes to a bad end.

In his latest film, *The Doom Generation* (1995), the first to have a major budget, Los Angeles teens are once again featured amid violence and sex. Two boys and a girl go off on a journey which, characteristically, leads nowhere. The seeming nihilism of so many of Araki's characters challenges viewers to confront their own mores, and though Araki's screenplays and direction often celebrate these teens' refusal to conform, the resulting films don't flinch from depicting the arid reality so many of these kids and young adults face.

Gregg Araki

An Early Frost

E

A groundbreaking, made-for-television movie that examines the dramatic consequences and abrasive personal conflicts that follow when parents discover their brilliant son (Aidan Quinn), a talented lawyer, is stricken with AIDS. Gena Rowlands and Ben Gazzara are the couple, alternately hurt, resentful and devastated. Sherman Yellen's story was adapted by Ron Cowen and Daniel Lipman. With Sylvia Sidney, D.W. Moffett and John Glover, who gives a searing supporting performance as a man fighting the disease.

VHS: S30446. $19.95.

John Erman, USA, 1985, 100 mins.

Edward II

Derek Jarman's brilliant, provocative adaptation of Christopher Marlowe's play about the rise and fall of the 15th-century ruler, Edward II (Steven Waddington). The indiscriminate king neglects his beautiful, ambitious wife (Tilda Swinton) to carry out an obsessive, homoerotic relationship with his military lieutenant (Andrew Tiernan). Through its stripped-down aesthetic, mobile camera work and striking parallels to contemporary life, *Edward II* is utterly convincing. Annie Lennox performs the sublime "Every Time We Say Goodbye." With Nigel Terry and Kevin Collins. Designed by Christopher Hobbs. Cinematography by Ian Wilson. Written by Jarman, Stephen McBride and Ken Butler.

VHS: S17626. $19.95.

Derek Jarman, Great Britain, 1991, 91 mins.

Ernesto

The Eighties

A bold musical set in a modern shopping mall, *The Eighties* is constructed in two parts. The first hour is shot on video; the last part is an opulent succession of musical numbers shot on 35mm. "Chantal Akerman's all-dancing, all-singing jigsaw puzzle is a musical in the way that *Stranger than Paradise* is a road film—it's an ironic, playful reworking (or disassembling) of a popular genre. Dense and fragmentary, the first hour of this film/video, fiction/documentary hybrid is culled from hours of rehearsal tapes. There's a cubist logic to Akerman's raw, sensuous montage which gloriously climaxes à la Busby Berkeley with a half-hour of lavish production numbers. Akerman tackles one of the oldest cliches of movie musical comedies—namely that of putting on a show—turns it inside out, and gives it a new lease on life" (J. Hoberman). French with English subtitles.
VHS: S12610. $79.95.
Chantal Akerman, Belgium/France, 1983, 85 mins.

El Diputado

A political/sexual thriller about a high-ranking homosexual member of the Spanish Socialist Party, *El Diputado* is based on an actual incident. A teenage hustler is set up by Spain's secret police to entrap the prominent politician. But the hustler discovers that he is falling in love with the man he must betray. "Superb! Exciting, intensely erotic visual cinema." (L.A. Times). Spanish with English subtitles.
VHS: S00397. $79.95.
Eloy de la Iglesia, Spain, 1983, 111 mins.

Empty Bed

Constructed in flashbacks, this thoughtful work is a drama about an aging gay man who reflects on the vigor and potency of his youth and who questions the choices he made in life. As he faces aging, he is distraught over the prospect of being alone yet finds it difficult to commit.
VHS: S14155. $29.95.
Mark Gasper, USA, 1990, 60 mins.

An Englishman Abroad

John Schlesinger's moody, ironic piece was made for the BBC. Set in the late 50s, the film is an account of a talented English theater actress (Coral Brown, based on her experiences) who meets and develops a strange bond with the exiled British spy Guy Burgess (Alan Bates) during a cultural exchange in Moscow. A quiet meditation on friendship, honor, politics and class, the film astutely examines Burgess' outlawed homosexuality and the pressures that drove him to betrayal.

VHS: S14328. Currently out of print. May be available for rental in some video stores.

John Schlesinger, Great Britain, 1983, 60 mins.

Entertaining Mr. Sloane

Joe Orton's macabre sexual farce is adapted for the cinema with its essential plot undisturbed. A nymphomaniac (Beryl Reid) and her repressed gay brother (Harry Andrews) stage an elaborate seduction of a handsome lodger/hustler (Peter McEnery) who is forced through circumstances into an extensive stay at their home. Cinematography by Wolfgang Suschitsky. Adaptation by Clive Exton. With Alan Webb.

VHS: S00409. Currently out of print. May be available for rental in some video stores.

Douglas Hickox, Great Britain, 1969, 94 mins.

Entre Nous

Diane Kurys' passionate work about the complicated relationship between two middle-class French women who are suffocating from the imprisonment and loneliness of their subservient roles. Set in Lyon in 1950, the film's textured, multilayered stories beautifully intersect. Isabelle Huppert and Miou Miou break away from their weak, insufferable husbands and develop an intense dependency. A closing title card reveals the story is about Kurys' mother. "Without resorting to melodrama, [the film shows] the desire and heartbreak of everyday life" (Time Out). With Guy Marchand, Jean-Pierre Bacri, Robin Renucci and Patrick Bauchau. French with English subtitles.

VHS: S00410. Currently out of print. May be available for rental in some video stores.

Diane Kurys, France, 1983, 100 mins.

Ernesto

Set in Trieste in 1911, Ernesto is the coming-of-age story of 17-year old Ernesto, the son of a prominent bourgeois family who dreams of being a violinist. His chance encounter with Ilio, a handsome violin student, blossoms into a love affair which is complicated by the amorous advances of Ilio's twin sister. Michele Placido won the Best Actor Award at the 1979 Berlin Film Festival. "Genuinely erotic and lushly mounted...the most complex rendition of homosexuality yet to reach the screen." (Richard Goldstein, *Village Voice*). Cinematography by Camillo Bazzoni. Written by Samperi, Barbara Alberti and Amadeo Paganini. Italian with English subtitles.
VHS: S00416. $49.95.
Salvatore Samperi, Italy, 1979, 98 mins.

Erotikus: History of the Gay Movie

This compilation program addresses the history of the male gay film. Its snippets progress from the early crude films of posed muscle-boys to sexually explicit works featuring male nudity and finally the hard-core films of recent vintage. Narrated by Fred Halsted. 54 mins.
VHS: S02168. $29.95.

Et l'Amour

This poetic vignette features two women engaged in a sensuous and tasteful erotic interlude. There is no dialog. 24 mins.
VHS: S27449. $24.95.

Eternal Return

Jean Cocteau retold the Tristan and Isolde legend within a contemporary context, set during the German Occupation. A young man (Jean Marais) tries to orchestrate a relationship between his friend (Madeleine Sologne) and a recently widowed uncle (Jean Murat), only to have his plan subverted by a vicious dwarf, who injects the couple with a love potion that seals their fate. Cinematography by Roger Hubert. Music by Georges Auric. With Yvonne de Bray, Pieral and Roland Toutain. French with English subtitles.
VHS: S04914. $29.95.
Jean Delannoy, France, 1943, 111 mins.

Everlasting Secret Family

This kinky Australian film centers on a prominent Australian politician who maintains a secret life of homosexual intrigue; he is the organizer of a secret society that recruits young men from exclusive private boys' schools. The clandestine existence involves him in a love affair with a student that leads into associations that threaten the Senator's career. *Everlasting Secret Family* is an odd mixture of homophobia and explicit sex. "Gleefully perverse! An invigorating mix of cinematic caprice and slyly creepy fun" (Seattle Times). With Arthur Dignam, Mark Lee and Heather Mitchell.

VHS: S14293. $79.95.

Michael Thornhill, Australia, 1989, 93 mins.

Everlasting Secret Family

F

Fearless Vampire Killers or: Pardon Me, But Your Teeth Are in My Neck

Roman Polanski's ambitious vampire horror movie melds gothic settings with elegance and deadpan wit. A determined but inept professor and his assistant are after an aristocratic family of Slavonic vampires but the ghouls' ambivalent sexual preferences throw them off track. The gay vampire who attacks Polanksi is one of the film's highlights. "An engaging oddity [with] long stretches that might have been lifted intact from any Hammer horror" (Tom Milne). Alternate title is *Dance of the Vampires*. Cinematography by Douglas Slocombe. Written by Gerard Brach and Polanski. Music by Krzysztof Komeda. With Polanski, Jack MacGowran, Sharon Tate, Alfie Bass and Ronald Lacey.

VHS: S12741. $19.98.
Roman Polanski, Great Britain, 1967, 124 mins.

Fellini Satyricon

Federico Fellini's operatic adaptation of Petronius Arbiter's witty story concerns sexual excursions into pre-Christian Rome, 500 BC. The plot centers on the conflicting lives and flamboyant exhibitions of two brilliant rivals with a manic flair for seeking out spectacle and pleasure. Virtually anything goes in this beautifully designed epic set in a decadent ancient Rome. Cinematography by Giuseppe Rotunno. Nino Rota worked on the score. With Martin Potter, Hiram Keller, Capucine and Luigi Montefiori. English dubbed.

VHS: S06318. $19.98.
Laser: Widescreen. LD70979. $124.95.
Federico Fellini, Italy, 1969, 138 mins.

Female Trouble

John Waters' low-budget masterpiece is an unsparing critique of middle American conformity and sexual oppression framed through a mock documentary on the squalid life and epic debauchery of Dawn Davenport (Divine). After a string of disappointments and personal failures, Dawn turns to criminal pursuits, adopting an elaborate series of impersonations—as mother, killer, model and pervert. The most disquieting sequence features Divine performing two roles simultaneously, of rapist and victim. With David Lochary, Mary Vivian

Fearless Vampire Killers or: Pardon Me, But Your Teeth Are in My Neck

Pearce, Mink Stole and Edith Massey.

VHS: S00439. Currently out of print. May be available for rental in some video stores.

John Waters, USA, 1974, 95 mins.

Fertile La Toyah Jackson Video Magazine: The Kinky Issue!

Fertile La Toyah Jackson is the perfect transy host for this look at a darker, and infinitely more interesting, side of L.A. glamour. It's violent and obscene, and also features appearances by Karen Black, Raquel Welch, Faye Dunaway, Billy Idol, Vaginal Davis, Jean Paul Gaultier, Peter Berlin, Joe Delassandro and other personalities. Jackson is the only video idol with a black dildo atop her head!

VHS: 29001. $39.95.

Fight for Us

Lino Brocka's powerful and courageous denunciation of the political situation in his home country of the Philippines. Philip Salvador, Dina Bonnevie, Gina Alajar and Bembol Roco star in this drama of a priest and social activist who is jailed under the old Marcos regime and emerges from prison only to challenge the new order of then-President Aquino. Tagalog with English subtitles.

VHS: S11900. Currently out of print. May be available for rental in some video stores.

Lino Brocka, Philippines, 1989, 92 mins.

The Films of Barbara Hammer

A pioneer of independent and experimental filmmaking, Barbara Hammer's films are unique for their personal investigations of sexuality and their sometimes breathtaking integration of documentary and experimental techniques.

Lesbian Humor

Six films by Barbara Hammer: *Menses* is a wry comedy on the disagreeable aspects of menstruation; the comedy *Superdyke* follows a troop of shield-bearing Amazons; *Our Trip* is an animated work considering the episodes of a hiking trip in the Andes; *Sync Touch* is an experimental film series that poses an aesthetic connection between touch and sight; *Doll House* is a rapid montage of objects arranged in relation to a doll house's central prop; and *No No Nooky TV* challenges the feminist controversy on the connection between sexuality and the electronic image and representation. "Hammer's satiric use of technology corresponds well with the '80s repression of sexual expression. If you've ever looked up 'lesbian' in a computer thesaurus, you'll know that it's not listed" (Independent Media).
VHS: S08608. $59.95.
Barbara Hammer, 1975-87, USA, 59 mins.

Lesbian Sexuality

A collection of four films by Barbara Hammer, featuring the landmark *Dyketactics*, a self-described "erotic lesbian commercial." The program also includes *Multiple Orgasm*, a sensually explicit film; *Double Strength*, a poetic study of a relationship between two trapeze artists; and *Women I Love*, which uses the camera as an extension of the body.
VHS: S08609. $59.95.
Barbara Hammer, USA, 1974-76, 57 mins.

Optical Nerves

Films by Barbara Hammer that "investigate the nature of spectator perception in an unfamiliar environment." *Optic Nerve* is a personal exploration of family and aging. *Place Mattes* explores the subtle balance experienced through reaching and touching, visualized through animation and optical printing techniques. *Endangered* is an experimental essay about the technological decline of light and film.
VHS: S08611. $59.95.
Barbara Hammer, USA, 1984-88, 44 mins.

Perceptual Landscapes

Four works that explore personal landscapes. Made in collaboration with Barbara Klutinis, *Pools* is a kaleidoscopic look at two swimming pools designed by the first woman architect in the United States. *Pond and Waterfall* identifies verdant pond growth interwoven with shots of dynamic light and water reflections. *Stone Circles* is a celebration of ancient, pre-patriarchal standing mounds and circles, including Stonehenge and Asbury. *Bent Time* is one of Hammer's most ambitious films, an attempt to "render visually the scientific theory that time, like rays, curves at the outer edges of the universe" (*Los Angeles Times*).

VHS: S08610. $59.95.

Barbara Hammer, USA, 1981-83, 54 mins.

The Films of James Broughton

In a remarkable career spanning more than 40 years, James Broughton has been one of the most articulate yet subtle voices in avant-garde American filmmaking. He's undisputably a master at fusing spoken poetry with moving and animated images. A poet and dramatist, Broughton has fused all three forms (film, poetry and drama) into what Stan Brakhage calls "an art of lifelong montage."

Autobiographical Mysteries

Testament (1974) is an exquisite self-portrait in which the poet/filmmaker contemplates his life and work through a rich and stylized assemblage of personal imagery, songs, anecdotes and dreams. *Devotions* (1983) is one of Broughton's vibrant collaborations with Joel Singer. The work casually envisions a time and place where men have abandoned all sexual rivalries in favor of homoerotic devotion, as 45 different couples discuss the ecstasy and pleasures men experience together. *Scattered Remains* (1988) is a performance piece in collaboration with Singer. It's a multifaceted portrait of Broughton performing his poems in a variety of unlikely situations. 57 mins.

VHS: S07287. $29.95.

The Films of James Broughton

The Films of James Broughton

Dreamwood

A spiritual odyssey into the ethereal landscape of the dream in which a mythical poet tries to reclaim his soul and set in motion his rebirth. "*Dreamwood* recreates the world of dream in time and space using...symbols and archetypes of the Unconscious for each step in the journey toward selfhood" (Freude Bartlett). Cinematography by John Schofill and Fred Padula. Music by Morton Subotnick.

VHS: S01575. $29.95.

James Broughton, USA, 1972, 45 mins.

Erotic Celebrations

Broughton's 1968 masterpiece, *The Bed*, is a lyrical, daring celebration of the immense physical, mental and erotic possibilities of action contained within a single plane—the bed. It is performed by an all-nude cast that includes some of San Francisco's best-known artists. *Erogeny* (1976) is an intimate examination of the body's contours and landscape. *Hermes Bird* (1979) and *Song of the Godbody* (1977) represent Broughton's subversion of sexual taboos, celebrating the ecstasy of physical awareness realized through close-up camera work. 47 mins.

VHS: S07284. $29.95.

Parables of Wonder

High Kukus (1973) visualizes Zen instructional techniques accompanied by 14 of Broughton's cuckoo haikus. *Golden Positions* (1978) is a series of tableaux vivants using the form of a liturgical service. *This Is It* (1971) is a playful, Zen-like myth shot in a home-movie style, featuring a two-year-old Adam in a backyard Eden. *The Gardener of Eden* (1981) is an intense, poetic work that honors the sexual dance of all creation, set in exotic, mysterious Sri Lanka. *Water Circle* (1975) is an homage to Lao-Tzu in a vibrant poem read by Broughton, with music by Corelli. 56 mins.

VHS: S07288. $29.95.

The Pleasure Garden

This comic fantasia is an off-beat tribute to British idiosyncracies, celebrating the triumph of love and personal expression over the forces of restriction and repression. A romantic, decaying park lies under the iron-fisted rule of a puritanical minister of public behavior who's obsessed with repressing the public's opportunities for love and emotional ecstasy. Produced by Lindsay Anderson. Cinematography by Walter Lassally. With Hattie Jacques, John Le Mesurier, Diana Maddox and Jean Anderson. 38 mins.

VHS: S07286. $29.95.

Rituals of Play

This collection of Broughton's three early black and white films is highlighted by his classic *Mother's Day* (1948). The film is an ironic recollection of childhood games filtered through the nostalgic textures of a cluttered family album. *Four in the Afternoon* (1951) stitches together four poetic variations on an intense longing and search for love and fulfillment. *Loony Tom* (1951) captures the amorous progress of an amiable tramp who seduces every woman he meets. 48 mins.

VHS: S07285. $29.95.

The Films of James Broughton

The complete 6-volume set.

VHS: S07289. $149.75.

The Films of Kenneth Anger

"One of the key figures of the postwar American avant-garde, Kenneth Anger's work is relatively free of the independent film circles and movements which his own work managed to anticipate in almost every case.... Anger embodies the 'radical otherness' of the avant-garde filmmaker, casting himself not only outside the mainstream, but as its negative image" (Ed Lowry). Many may know Anger as the author of *Hollywood Babylon*.

Fireworks

This collection includes *Fireworks*, which follows the cruising adventures of a young man (Anger) and a sailor; *Rabbit's Moon*, a fable about the unattainable combining elements of Commedia dell'Arte with Japanese myth; and *Eaux d'Artifice*, which deals with a masked and costumed figure who enigmatically moves through the fountains of the Tivoli gardens.

VHS: S00800. $29.95.

Kenneth Anger, USA, 1947-55, 34 mins.

Inauguration of the Pleasure Dome

Anger described this as a "convocation of magicians who assume the identity of gods and goddesses in a Dionysian revel.... Dedicated to the few and to Aleister Crowley, and the crowned and conquering child." One of the most impressive works of American experimental cinema.

VHS: S00801. $29.95.

Kenneth Anger, USA, 1954, 38 mins.

Lucifer Rising

This program features *Invocation of My Demon Brother*, about conjuring up pagan forces, constructed from outtakes of Anger's first version of *Lucifer Rising*, his uncompleted opus that was interrupted when the print was stolen by an artist involved with the film. With music by Mick Jagger. The program also features Anger's alternate version of *Lucifer Rising* (1974), filmed primarily in Egypt—a dense and evocative intermixing of experimental shots. It's a film "about the love generation, the birthday party of the Aquarian Age, showing actual ceremonies to make Lucifer rise" (Anger).
VHS: S00802. $29.95.
Kenneth Anger, USA, 1969, 39 mins.

Scorpio Rising

Kenneth Anger's masterpiece is "a tour-de-force collage of pop imagery. It's a paean to the American motorcyclist, a revelation of the violent, homoerotic undercurrent of American culture, and a celebration of the forces of chaos in the universe" (Ed Lowry). Filmed in Brooklyn and Manhattan, and at Walden Pond, the film is structured in four parts. The director described the film as "a conjuration of the Presiding Princes, Angels and Spirits of the Sphere of MARS, formed as a 'high' view of the Myth of the American Motorcyclist." With music by Ricky Nelson, Little Peggy March, The Angels, Bobby Vinton, The Crystals, The Ran-Dells and Kris Jensen. With Bruce Byron, Johnny Sapienza, Frank Carifi and John Paline.
VHS: The film is currently unavailable because of litigation over music rights.
Kenneth Anger, USA, 1963-64, 29 mins.

Flesh

Paul Morrissey's underground epic stars Joe Dallesandro as a charming, naive innocent who turns to street hustling in order to finance his wife's lover's abortion. He meets a succession of grotesque street characters, including an artist with elaborate theories about body worship, a group of transvestites, a dumb ex-girlfriend (now a topless dancer), and a friend whose armpits have been burned by a flamethrower. The whole exercise is "hilarious, poignant and real" (*Los Angeles Herald-Examiner*). With Geraldine Smith, Patti D'Arbanville and Maurice Bradell.
VHS: S06250. Currently out of print. May be available for rental in some video stores.
Paul Morrissey, USA, 1968, 90 mins.

Fellini Satyricon

Flickers

Theatrical trailers from some of the most intriguing gay-themed films are collected into this feature presentation. *Caligula, Sebastiane, Prick Up Your Ears, My Beautiful Launderette, Cabaret, Nijinsky, The Ritz, The Gay Deceivers* and other classic film previews offer surprising entertainment. 91 mins.

VHS: S27611. $24.95.

The Flower of My Secret

From the acclaimed director of *Tie Me Up! Tie Me Down!* and *Women on the Verge of a Nervous Breakdown* comes this fun story of a romance writer, fresh out of inspiration, who goes looking for a little real-life love of her own. Starring Marisa Paredes, Juan Echanove, Carmen Elias, Rossy de Palma and Chus Lampreave. "Delicious! Funny! Almodovar returns to the comedy of his earlier, best work" (Caryn James, *The New York Times*). "Funny and smart, but with heart!" (Jay Carr, *The Boston Globe*). Spanish with English subtitles.

VHS: S30148. $97.99.
Laser: LD75995. $39.95.
Pedro Almodovar, Spain, 1996, 101 mins.

Forbidden Passion

Michael Gambon stars as the remarkable poet, novelist, playwright, scholar and wit Oscar Wilde—a man of enormous charm and talent who was both celebrated and reviled. This film centers around Wilde's explosive and socially illicit sex triangle; the plot details his voracious sexual appetites and the highly repressive Victorian establishment that punished him for his outlawed relationship with Lord Alfred Douglas.

VHS: S05895. $79.95.

Henry Herbert, Great Britain, 1976, 120 mins.

Forever Mary

Set in a rigid reformatory in Palermo, Sicily, *Forever Mary* concerns the struggles of an idealistic schoolteacher who tries to ease the pain and hardship faced by its inmates. The social and sexual dynamics are thrown off stride with the appearance of Mary, a teenage transvestite prostitute who is assigned to the school. With Michele Placido, Alessandro DiSanzo and Francesco Benigno. Italian with English subtitles.

VHS: S15443. $79.95.

Marco Risi, Italy, 1991, 100 mins.

Fortune and Men's Eyes

A stark, controversial adaptation of John Herbert's play about homosexual life inside a prison cell. Brutal and uncompromising in its time, now its portrayal of homoerotic desire behind bars may strike some as camp. "A powerful and often shocking film" (*Newsweek*). With Wendell Burton, Michael Greer and Zooey (David) Hall.

VHS: S17657. $19.98.

Harvey Hart, Canada, 1971, 102 mins.

Fortune and Men's Eyes

Fox and His Friends

Rainer Werner Fassbinder's caustic essay charts the fortunes of Fox (played by Fassbinder), a lower-class carnival entertainer whose quest for love and acceptance leads him to invest his massive lottery earnings into the family-run business of his elegant bourgeois lover. This ill-fated romance between "the capitalist and the lottery queen" results in one of Fassbinder's most skillfully wrought films, expertly evoking a brittle, upper-class, gay milieu where, as one character puts it, "God's dressed up like Marlene Dietrich, holding his nose." Cinematography by Michael Ballhaus. With Peter Chatel, Harry Baer and Ulla Jacobsson. German with English subtitles.
VHS: S06443. $79.95.
Rainer W. Fassbinder, W. Germany, 1975, 123 mins.

Fried Green Tomatoes

Jon Avnet's film is a fresh, sentimental adaptation of comedienne Fannie Flagg's novel *Fried Green Tomatoes at the Whistle Stop Cafe*, juxtaposing two distinct narratives. The first is a contemporary work about the relationship of an abused, self-loathing woman (Kathy Bates) and a staunchly independent, sharp octagenarian (Jessica Tandy). Tandy interweaves stories of her friendship with a young woman in the pre-World War II South. With intense, heartfelt performances from Mary Stuart Masterson and Mary-Louise Parker. Barbara Ling's production design and Geoffrey Simpson's burnished cinematography beautifully establish the textures, atmosphere and place.
VHS: S17015. $19.98.
Jon Avnet, USA, 1991, 130 mins.

Friends Forever

A teenage boy's sexual confusion becomes a catalyst for change in this tender and unpredictable first feature. Kristian, a shy 16-year-old, is starting at a new school. An uncertain conformist, he is irresistibly drawn to two boys who dominate his class: Henrik, whose unyielding independence belies his androgynous sexual charisma, and Patrick—blond, boisterous and moody—who leads a tyrannical band of troublemakers. The boys' friendship instills self-confidence in Kristian, but their relationship is soon put to the test. Danish with English subtitles.
VHS: S15821. $69.95.
Stefan Christian Henszelman, Denmark, 1986, 95 mins.

Frisk

Based on the novel by Dennis Cooper, this controversial, sensual and suggestive work is about fantasy, sexuality and how violence and pornography shape the human psyche. Punctuated with strobe flashes of layered S & M images, it unfolds in an elliptical style. Stars Michael Gunther, Craig Chester, Parker Posey, Alexis Arquette, Raoul O'Connell, Jaie Laplante, James Lyons, and Michael Stock. "...a serious and discreet work of considerable, dark impact—and no little humor" (Kevin Thomas, *Los Angeles Times*).
VHS: S30136. $59.99.
Todd Verow, USA, 1996, 84 mins.

Fun Down There

Buddy is a young man living with his ordinary family in upstate New York. His only source of sexual gratification is between the covers of *Playgirl* magazine. Finally Buddy leaves the small town, heads for New York City, and during his first week in the East Village finds a job, new friends, (safe) sexual adventure, and perhaps romance. "It's one of the more accomplished gay narratives to emerge since Bill Sherwood's *Parting Glances....* I'm ready for the sequel" (Karl Soehnein, *The Village Voice*). With Michael Waite, Nickolas Nagourney, Gretschen Somerville and Martin Goldin.
VHS: S13508. $39.95.
Roger Stigliano, USA, 1988, 89 mins.

Friends Forever

The talented director **Lino Brocka** (1940-1991) was the most important international figure in Filipino cinema. The son of a fisherman and teacher, he was born in San Jose, Neuvo Ecija, the Philippines. After graduating from the University of the Philippines, he converted to Mormonism and was sent as a missionary to serve at a leper colony in Hawaii. Following a number of conflicts with church authorities, Brocka left the church and traveled throughout the United States. He returned home to work as a script supervisor on Monte Hellman's low-budget, locally produced *Flight to Fury* (1966). Brocka went on to work in television and direct plays for the Philippine Educational Theatre Association.

In 1970 Brocka made the transition to feature filmmaking with *Wanted: Perfect Mother*, the first of eight "komiks" novels, serialized, popular works that he transformed into lavish and opulent melodramas. In 1974, he formed his own production company, Cine Manila, enabling him to make more substantial, critical films. Brocka promptly turned out his most significant early work, *Manila in the Claws of Night* (1975), a dark, gritty depiction of the experiences of youths arriving from the country to face urban corruption and vice.

Brocka was largely unknown in the West, until the 1978 Cannes Film Festival, when *Insiang* was shown to great international acclaim. *Insiang* was the first film in Brocka's important trilogy—which included *Jaguar* (1979) and *Bona* (1980)—that explored Manila's impoverished shantytowns. With the trilogy, Brocka's films took a more overtly political turn. He became a relentless critic of the Marcos regime, actively challenging government censorship while documenting the devastating social conditions and plight of the poor.

With the collapse of Cine Manila in the late '70s, Brocka turned out a number of potboilers, melodramas, juvenile delinquent movies and social dramas in order to finance his more challenging works. *Macho Dancer* (1988), his first explicitly gay work, examines the exploitation of gay bar dancers, focusing on a young strip-tease artist who befriends a street hustler and a prostitute. Brocka followed that film with *Fight for Us* (1989), a powerful denunciation of the endemic corruption of contemporary Filipino politics. Brocka's later films drew attention to the continuity and transfer of corruption from the Marcos to Aquino governments.

Brocka's last film, *Dirty Affair* (1990), concerns a Marcos-like mayor who sexually enslaves a psychologically unbalanced film star, involving her in a campaign of dirty tricks and covert assassinations. The film combined Brocka's usual preoccupations with a heightened visual style, an over-the-top theatricality and a kinetic pace. Stylistically, Brocka drew on a wide range of influences, including Italian neorealism, American film noir and the melodramatic conventions of the Spanish soap opera. In a 1983 interview, Brocka said, "The reason my films are melodramas, film noir, is because I love them—I love John Garfield movies with all those wet streets, and film noir seems to me to be close to the social reality of the Philippines. I have always been in love with the characters. They are terminal people, pushed against the wall— they have nowhere to go. But they don't give up. They turn around, away from the wall. They make a choice. They're strong. They fight back."

Brocka made nearly 50 films in 20 years before his death in a car accident, in Manila, in May of 1991. The late German-born documentarian Christian Blackwood made a documentary about the filmmaker called *Signed, Lino Brocka* (1987).

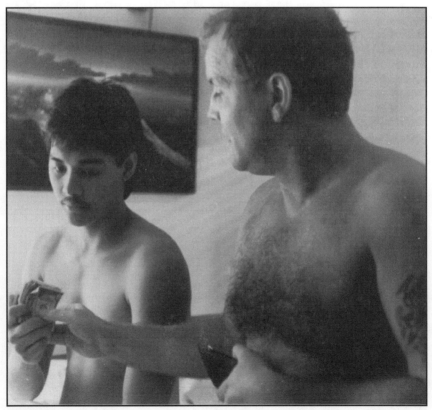

Macho Dancer

The Gay Deceivers

G

An elaborate hoax film about two good-looking thrill-seekers who avoid military service by pretending to be homosexuals. The farce gets really complicated when the pair moves into a gay apartment complex, setting in motion a succession of deceptive acts.

VHS: S02221. $59.95.
Bruce Kessler, USA, 1968, 97 mins.

Gay for a Day

Two documentaries from Chicago-based independent filmmaker Tom Palazzolo. *Gay for a Day* chronicles the defiant spirit of the 1976 Chicago Gay Pride Parade. *Costumes in Review* is a humorous, shrewd look at a festive gay costume party.

VHS: S06112. $39.95.
Tom Palazzolo, USA, 45 mins.

Geek Maggot Bingo

An unclassifiable work created by Nick Zedd, the unofficial leader of the gay New York underground "Cinema of Transgression." The film is a horror spoof that's a perverse collection of in-jokes and a monument to bad taste. Donna Death plays Scumbalina, a vampire queen. Richard Hell plays an alternative punk rocker with a flair for country music. Cookie Mueller described the film as a "breath of fresh air, but infected with bats, flies and spawning maggots." Special effects by Ed French. With Brenda Bergman and John Zacherle.

VHS: S10163. $39.95.
Nick Zedd, USA, 1983, 70 mins.

Gender: The Enduring Paradox

Gender's role in contemporary society is being challenged by a number of new trends. This video examines the roots of traditional gender in early childhood and the socially constructed roles arising to define masculinity and feminity. 58 mins.
VHS: S29541. $19.98.

Glitter Goddess of the Sunset Strip

Girl Friends

Claudia Weill's breakthrough feature about an apprentice art photographer who is forlorn when her roommate gets married and moves out. She is replaced by a gay dance freak who creates turmoil when she borrows a blouse. One of the film's pioneering features is its appraisal of lesbianism as a fair life option. With Melanie Mayron, Anita Skinner, Eli Wallach and Christopher Guest.

VHS: S03714. $19.95.

Claudia Weill, USA, 1978, 88 mins.

The Glass Menagerie

Paul Newman's naturalistic adaptation of Tennessee Williams' Southern gothic about the moral and spiritual dissolution of the Wingfield family. The action is confined to their St. Louis apartment at the height of the Depression. The movie deals with the delusions of former Southern aristocrat Amanda (Joanne Woodward), her emotionally unsettled daughter Laura (Karen Allen) and her pathetically weak son Tom (John Malkovich). James Naughton contributes a stunning turn as the gentleman caller. "The acting is bruisingly true; the deep guilt of family is present throughout; everybody feels martyred. Newman trusts the words to conjure up the old crushed magnolia" (*Time Out*).

VHS: S07142. $19.98.
Laser: LD70032. $39.98.

Paul Newman, USA, 1987, 134 mins.

Glitter Goddess of the Sunset Strip

Llana Lloyd's autobiographical memoir about her sexual ambiguity, self-definition, and a life that reads like a camp melodrama. Created from Super-8mm home movie footage and period recreations, Lloyd assesses the complicated emotional repercussions of her domineering mother's militant lesbianism. "Mentally intense and satirical, this psycho shocker is shaped to emphasize the fascinating and fragile imperfections of human kind" (*Film Threat Magazine*). With Diane Nelson.

VHS: S18744. $69.99.

Dick Campbell, USA, 1992, 120 mins.

Gods of the Plague

Rainer Werner Fassbinder's engaging third feature combines the melancholia and despair of the European action movie, the self-

---

reflexive irony of the French New Wave and the gritty allure and terse style of the American B-movie. Two losers, a career criminal (Harry Baer) and his unbalanced comrade (Gunther Kaufmann), orchestrate a supermarket heist. Their plans crumble under the cruel machinations of two women (Hanna Schygulla and Margarethe von Trotta) who are hopelessly attracted to Baer. Cinematography by Dietrich Lohmann. German with English subtitles.
VHS: S11149. $29.95.
Rainer W. Fassbinder, W. Germany, 1970, 91 mins.

The Gospel According to St. Matthew

Pasolini's second feature film is arguably the finest interpretation of the Christ story, a literal approach which portrays Christ as an anguished preacher against social injustice. Pasolini uses the rugged landscapes of southern Italy, non-actors, imagery from Italian masters, including Giotto and Piero della Francesca, and music ranging from Bach to Billie Holiday to depict the birth, life, meaning and violent death of Christ. Cinematography by Tonino delli Colli. With Enrique Irazoqui, Susanna Pasolini, Mario Socrate and Marcello Morante. Italian with English subtitles.
VHS: S18168. $29.95.
Pier Paolo Pasolini, Italy, 1964, 136 mins.

Gothic

Ken Russell's bizarre, frightening meditation on the possible sexual and artistic interactions among a group of writers and artists on June 16, 1816, at the Villa Diodati. The film explores the emotional connections and erotic scenarios unfolding between Lord Byron, Shelley, his lover Mary Godwin and her half-sister Claire. With Gabriel Byrne, Miranda Richardson, Myrian Cyr and Julian Sands.
VHS: S04624. $14.98.
Ken Russell, Great Britain, 1987, 90 mins.

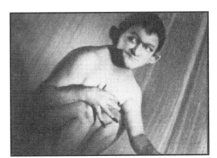

Girl Friends　　　　　　　　　　　*Gothic*

Hairspray

John Waters' breakthrough commercial work is a witty, extremely well-made piece of mock nostalgia. The frenetic storyline traces the efforts of a politically conscious white girl to integrate a local television bandstand in 1962 Baltimore. This was Waters' first mainstream hit, though it's memorable as Waters' final collaboration with Divine. Waters' growth as a filmmaker is visible in a shrewd use of color and a shock editing style reminiscent of early Russ Meyer films. With Ricki Lake, Sonny Bono, Debbie Harry, Pia Zadora and Ric Ocasek.
VHS: S07303. $14.98.
John Waters, USA, 1988, 96 mins.

Happily Ever After

From the director of *Dona Flor and Her Two Husbands*, *Happily Ever After* stars Regina Duarte as an apparently satisfied Brazilian housewife who drifts into a passionate affair with Miguel, a bisexual transvestite. Miguel introduces Duarte into a seamy, alluring criminal underworld; it's an alternately vibrant, frightening milieu that shatters her middle-class complacency. With Paul Castelli. Portuguese with English subtitles.
VHS: S06014. $69.95.
Bruno Barreto, Brazil, 1986, 106 mins.

Hawks and Sparrows

Pier Paolo Pasolini's comic fable concerns the misadventures of a father and son who renounce their privileged upbringing to lead a nomadic existence. They undertake a mythic quest to re-enact St. Francis of Assisi's mission with the birds. The film's dialectic posits the conflict between the Church and Marxism, individuals and the state. The gifted, stone-faced clown Toto represents the Everyman. Cinematography by Mario Bernardo and Tonino Delli Colli. Music by Ennio Morricone and Domenico Modugno. With Ninetto Davoli, Rossana Di Rocco, Renato Capogna and Pietro Davoli. Italian with English subtitles.
VHS: S12351. $29.95.
Pier Paolo Pasolini, Italy, 1964, 88 mins.

Heat

Andy Warhol's offbeat remake of Billy Wilder's *Sunset Boulevard*, directed by his protege Paul Morrissey. Sylvia Miles is an obscure actress attracted to game shows, television movies and narcissistic hustlers. The endlessly hip, ruthlessly vain Joe Dallesandro plays a former child actor living in a decrepit motel. His unconventional life is ruled over by a bizarre landlady who complains about her daughter's unconventional nuclear family, replete with baby daughter and lesbian lover. The film trafficks in "high comedy and low tragedy...with a gifted and offbeat cast" (Judith Crist). With Andrea Feldman, Pat Ast and Ray Vestal. Produced by Andy Warhol.

VHS: S00553. Currently out of print. May be available for rental in some video stores.

Paul Morrissey, USA, 1972, 102 mins.

Heaven's a Drag

Mark and Simon, two men in love, are suddenly separated by AIDS and death. Undone by grief, Simon tries to blot out his intense emotions by diving into the swinging life of a gay bachelor. His deceased ex, a former drag artist, is horrified by Simon's actions and refuses to enter Heaven until he is sure that his memory will live on. That means any prospective new paramour of Simon's will have to deal with a queer, territorial ghost.

VHS: S27429. $59.95.

Peter Mackenzie Litten, Great Britain, 1995, 96 mins.

Henry & June

Philip Kaufman's intelligent portrait of the love triangle between author Henry Miller, his wife June and Anaïs Nin was adapted from Nin's private journals. Kaufman captures the sexual and intellectual freedom of '30s Paris café society through casual, clever sketches. Henry and Anaïs rely on June's sexual independence for artistic creation, until the strain and demands lead to June's breakdown. The film is a meditation on the complicated relations of the body and the mind. Cinematography by Philippe Rousselot. With Fred Ward, Uma Thurman, Maria de Medeiros and Richard E. Grant.

VHS: S13578. $19.98.

Philip Kaufman, USA, 1990, 135 mins.

High Heels

Part revenge comedy, part thriller and sexual farce, Pedro Almodovar's *High Heels* is a melodrama about the bizarre and shifting relationship of an aging Spanish movie star and singer (Marisa Paredes) and her daughter, a prominent local television anchor woman (Victoria Abril). Estranged for more than 20 years, Paredes returns to Madrid to discover that Abril is married to one of Mom's former lovers (Feodor Atkine). His murder sets the extravagant plot in motion. Almodovar throws in virtually everything: an acrobatic sex scene, a score of transsexuals, a bizarre prison dance number, a buried family secret and an on-camera confession. With Miguel Bose and Bibi Anderssen. Cinematography by Alberto Mayo. Score by Ryuichi Sakamoto (*The Last Emperor*). Spanish with English subtitles.
VHS: S16919. $89.95.
Pedro Almodovar, Spain, 1990, 115 mins.

Home for the Holidays

Holly Hunter, Robert Downey, Jr., Dylan McDermott, Anne Bancroft, Claire Danes, Charles Durning, Geraldine Chaplin and Steve Guttenberg are the all-star cast of this family comedy. Hunter's character has troubles at work and at home, and just when it seems things can't get any worse for this Chicago art restoration expert, she heads to her parents' house for Thanksgiving. Her brother's gay, her sister and her husband are uptight, her aunt's a drunk and her parents are crazy, but at least it's home.
VHS: S27515. $19.95.
Laser: LD75523. $34.95.
Jodie Foster, USA, 1995, 103 mins.

The Hours and Times

Christopher Munch's feature debut is an impressionistic and speculative piece about the circumstances and possible sexual relationship between John Lennon and Beatles manager Brian Epstein during a four-day holiday in Barcelona during the spring of 1963. This delicate, heartbreaking film depicts the inner world of each man, evoking Epstein's erotic obsession and Lennon's confusion and pain as an emerging rock and roll icon. One of the best films ever made about unrequited love. Munch wrote, directed and photographed the film. With David Angus, Ian Hart and Stephanie Pack.
VHS: S18741. $19.98.
Christopher Munch, USA, 1991, 60 mins.

I Became a Lesbian and Others Too

Four shorts bring humor and insight to the lesbian experience. Included are *Just a Little Crush*, *I Became a Lesbian*, *Cat Nip* and *Le Poisson d'Amour*. From the girl next door to grandma's secret past, even amongst a bunch of cuddly kitties, who knows where lesbian desire can be found lurking? 52 mins.

VHS: S27757. $29.95.

I Like You, I Like You Very Much

This is one of the few sexually explicit films available from Japan. Yu has a nice college student boyfriend, but that does not stop him from approaching a sexy stranger waiting for a train one evening. There is only one thing he can say. "I like you; I like you very much." Japanese with English subtitles.

VHS: S29951. $39.95.

Oki Hiroyuki, Japan, 1994, 58 mins.

I Only Want You to Love Me (Ich Will Doch Nur, Dass Ihr Mich Liebt)

Fassbinder crafts a striking tale about a young man who desires only to be loved. Unfortunately, he is saddled by debts and troubled by an unfulfilling home life. In this dark melodrama, his wife and parents seem indifferent to him and to his pain. His unhappy life is significantly altered for the worse when, one night, in a drunken stupor, he kills a bar-keeper, mistaking him for his distant father. German with English subtitles.

VHS: S27665. $39.95.

Rainer W. Fassbinder, West Germany, 1976, 100 mins.

I Shot Andy Warhol

Lili Taylor is Valerie Solanas, the eccentric writer of a play called *Up Your Ass* and the founder and sole member of the revolutionary group called the Society for Cutting Up Men (*SCUM*). This film shows Warhol's Factory through its heyday, until it all was radically changed by a furious, gun-toting Solanas. Her revenge against Warhol for refusing to produce her play sent shockwaves through the art world. Stephen Dorff is Candy Darling and Jared Harris is Warhol.

VHS: S29783. $99.99.

Mary Harron, USA, 1996, 100 mins.

I the Worst of All

Based on the book *Traps of Faith* by Nobel Prize winner Octavio Paz, this is the last film completed by Maria Luisa Bemberg (*Camilla, I Don't Want to Talk About It*) before her death in 1995. The film tells the story of real-life poet and writer Sister Juana Ines de la Cruz (Assumpta Serna, *Matador*), a target of the Spanish Inquisition, and her passionate relationship with a Viceroy's wife (Dominique Sanda, *The Conformist*), who protects the nun so that she may continue her work. As the Sister's status begins to grow, the Church attempts to silence the outspoken nun. Considered radical for her time, Sister Juana is now recognized as one of Mexico's greatest poets. Spanish with English subtitles.

VHS: S27733. $59.95.

Maria Luisa Bemberg, Argentina, 1993, 100 mins.

It's My Party

Eric Roberts stars as a young man diagnosed with AIDS who decides to throw a blow-out farewell party for himself in this inspirational celebration of love, life and friendship. All-star cast includes Margaret Cho, Lee Grant, Gregory Harrison, Marlee Matlin, Olivia Newton-John, Bronson Pinchot and George Segal.

VHS: S28498. $19.98.

Randal Kleiser, USA, 1995, 109 mins.

I've Heard the Mermaids Singing

A wonderfully whimsical tale about imagination and the rude intrusion of reality into the life of an awkward temp worker with a penchant for photography. Polly is the temp who gets a job in a chic Toronto gallery, where she develops a crush on her sophisticated boss. With Sheila McCarthy, Paule Baillargeon, Ann-Marie MacDonald and John Evans.

VHS: S06046. Currently out of print. May be available for rental in some video stores.

Patricia Rozema, Canada, 1987, 83 mins.

Images: A Lesbian Love Story

This sincere, low-budget film revolves around Claire and Dorie, a sexually satisfied couple whose six-year relationship, held together by mutual openness and candor, is tested by a new player. Alyx is a dynamic, sexually open, energetic lesbian enthralled by life, love and women. She is obsessively drawn to Claire. "At last, a woman-identified and realistic portrayal of women loving women" (*Lavender Press*).

VHS: S06032. $59.95.

Ruth Barrett/Cynthia Smith, USA, 1987, 54 mins.

Imogen Cunningham: Never Give Up

Ann Hershey's impressionistic, subtle biography of the remarkable photographer Imogen Cunningham, an artist who withstood the intense social and sexual oppression of early 20th-century American life to become one of the most incisive and distinctive portrait photographers of her era. Hershey's candid conversations with Cunningham, filmed when the artist was 92, make up the bulk of the film. Cunningham talks about her experiences of shooting Spencer Tracy, Cary Grant, Martha Graham and more than 70 other subjects.

VHS: S16833. $29.95.

Ann Hershey, USA, 1993, 30 mins.

The Importance of Being Earnest

An exquisitely performed adaptation of Oscar Wilde's classic farce about social convention and Victorian manners. The witty conceit concerns two wealthy men who conceal their backgrounds to seduce prospective marriage partners. Unfortunately, they encounter little success. Wilde's larger concern is to mercilessly subvert Victorian hypocrisy. Cinematography by Desmond Dickinson. Screenplay adaptation by Anthony Asquith. With Michael Redgrave, Michael Denison, Edith Evans, Margaret Rutherford and Joan Greenwood.

VHS: S06234. Currently out of print. May be available for rental in some video stores.

Anthony Asquith, Great Britain, 1952, 95 mins.

The Impostors

Improper Conduct

The Impostors

Mark Rappaport's breakthrough film stars the late, great Charles Ludlam of the Ridiculous Theater. The "dense and fascinating independent feature—a tragicomic melodrama designed to stick in the throat (and brain)—surely qualifies as one of the wildest and wittiest American movies of the decade. The structure is basically confrontational: gay and/or straight couples, twins and/or lovers, crooks and/or romantic heroes, doppelgangers all, try to ridicule one another out of existence, with enough deadpan bitchy dialog to choke a horse, and a plot derived equally from *The Maltese Falcon* and Proust's *Albertine disparue*.... Magic, stolen jewels, jealousy, paranoia, and torture parade through this hysterically convoluted, elegantly mounted tale of wisecracks and woe like a Hollywood procession for American romanticism: the results are nightmarish, hilarious, and indelible" (Jonathan Rosenbaum, *Chicago Reader*).
VHS: S31138. $29.99.
Mark Rappaport, USA, 1980, 110 mins.

Improper Conduct

The late cinematographer Nestor Almendros co-directed (with Orlando Jimenez-Leal) this powerful documentary about Fidel Castro's violent persecution of gays and intellectuals. Covering the 25 years of Castro's regime, the film uses interviews with 20 Cuban emigrés, exiles, gays, artists, poets, intellectuals and filmmakers to chronicle a highly repressive system that outlaws civil liberties and declares homosexuality a crime against the state. The film also attacks American and Cuban leftists' reluctance to condemn Castro's policies. Spanish with English subtitles.

VHS: S00614. $19.95.

Nestor Almendros/Orlando Jimenez-Leal, France, 1984, 112 mins.

In a Glass Cage

In this Spanish horror thriller, a young man insinuates himself into the family of the sadistic Nazi concentration camp doctor who sexually exploited him during World War II. Living in exile in Spain, the doctor is confined by an iron lung. The young man engineers a violent series of sadomasochistic sexual games against his former tormentor, playing out the chilling details related in the doctor's war-era diary. The film is a brutal and unyielding recreation of the horror and depravity visited on the young man. With Gunter Meisner, David Sust and Marisa Paredes. Spanish and German with English subtitles.

VHS: S10734. $79.95.

Agustin Villaronga, Spain, 1986, 110 mins.

In a Shallow Grave

A strange, unaccountable sexual chiller about a horribly disfigured soldier (Michael Biehn) who is awakened from his acute isolation by a nomadic, sensually alluring young man (Patrick Dempsey) who shows up at the man's decaying farmhouse. With Maureen Mueller, Michael Beach and Thomas Boyd Mason.

VHS: S08316. $19.98.

Kenneth Bowser, USA, 1988, 92 mins.

The Inheritors

A terrifying psychological drama about the resurgence of neofascism and xenophobia. A young man with a troubled home life and few economic opportunities finds comfort, respect and power within a violent neo-Nazi group. He's part of a vicious campaign to play out violent homoerotic impulses and ideas. With Nikolas Vogel, Roger Schauer, Klaus Novak and Johnanna Tomek. German with English subtitles.

VHS: S00624. Currently out of print. May be available for rental in some video stores.

Walter Bannert, Austria, 1984, 89 mins.

The Innocent

Luchino Visconti's last film is a somber work about sexual revenge and erotic obsession, adapted from Gabriele D'Annunzio's novel. Laura Antonelli avenges her wealthy Sicilian husband's (Giancarlo Giannini) infidelities by entering into a risky affair. "The film resolves itself into an almost painfully sincere meditation on masculine self-delusion" (*Time Out*). Cinematography by Pasqualino De Santis. With Jennifer O'Neill, Rina Morelli, Massimo Girotti and Didier Haudepin. Italian with English subtitles.

VHS: S00625. $29.95.
Luchino Visconti, Italy, 1976, 125 mins.

Is Lucyna a Girl? (Czy Lucyna to Dziewczyna?)

A revolutionary '30s Polish comedy starring Jadwiga Smosarska as a woman impersonating a man who's hired as an engineer. She beautifully conjures up her feminist sensibility to provoke her colleagues. Polish with *NO* subtitles.

VHS: S15571. $39.95.
Juliusz Gardan, Poland, 1934, 80 mins.

The Innocent

Je, Tu, Il, Elle

Chantal Akerman's first feature is composed in three episodes. In the first, the central character (Akerman) writes, reads aloud and re-arranges the furniture in her room. In the second, she goes out and meets a truck driver who fills her with stories of his life and its routine. Finally, she arrives at the home of her lover. The two women face an emotional gulf, but rather than talk about it, choose to make love. Sexually open yet abstracted, passionate yet distant, *Je, Tu, Il, Elle* is a remarkable exploration of lesbian, feminist space. With Niels Arestrup and Claire Wauthion. French with English subtitles.

VHS: S12562. $29.95.
Chantal Akerman, France, 1974, 90 mins.

Jean Cocteau: Autobiography of an Unknown

An engaging portrait of poet, writer, filmmaker and gay artist Jean Cocteau. Weaving together archival footage and memoirs, Cocteau describes his childhood, his artistic evolution and his rise to prominence within the French avant-garde. Cocteau also discusses his family and the inspiration and influence of his circle of friends, a circle which included Nijinsky, Diaghilev, Renoir, Pablo Picasso, Satie and Charlie Chaplin. 60 mins.

VHS: S07597. $19.95.

Jerker

Hugh Harrison adapts Robert Chesley's play, which could be described as a gay equivalent of Nicholson Baker's novel *Vox*. The work reveals the movements, rhythms and arc of an adult relationship between two men, which consists entirely of anonymous, intense telephone conversations. "Raw, honest and unapologetic in its portrayal of gay sexuality" (*The Philadelphia Gay News*). With Tom Wagner and Joseph Stachura. Cinematography by Ron Hamill.

VHS: S17118. $19.95.
Hugh Harrison, USA, 1991, 120 mins.

The Jim Bailey Experience

Combining elements of the outrageous and avant-garde, Jim Bailey has been on the cutting edge of drag performance. In this hip compilation tape, Bailey pulls out all the stops with his dead-on impersonations and photo layouts of Judy Garland, Barbra Streisand, Marilyn Monroe and Madonna.
VHS: S16916. $39.95.
Stephen Campbell, USA

Jubilee

An angel transports Queen Elizabeth I from the year 1578 to a post-punk, post-Thatcher wasteland where civilization is frozen and bands of teenage punks and Fascist police roam the streets. Buckingham Palace is a recording studio, the center of an entertainment empire controlled by the ruthless, all-powerful media czar Borgia Ginz. The anti-heroes of the film reflect Elizabeth's mirror image: Bod, the murderous leader of a crazy household; historian Amyl Nitrate; the pyromaniac Mad; the sex-obsessed actress Crabs; loving brothers Sphinx and Angel; and the artist Viv. With Jenny Runacre, Jordan, Little Nell and Toyah Wilcox. Music by Brian Eno, Adam and the Ants, Siouxsie and the Banshees and Wayne County. "One of the most original, bold and exciting features to have come out of England" (*Variety*).
VHS: S12676. $29.95.
Derek Jarman, Great Britain, 1978, 105 mins.

Just a Gigolo

David Hemmings' artistically ambitious work stars David Bowie as a Prussian veteran who seeks employment in Berlin in the aftermath of World War I. He's trapped by harsh extremes, pursued alternately by homosexual fascists and lonely, wealthy widows. Bowie tries in vain to fight off his lethargic anguish and find some purpose and meaning in his life. The film was drastically cut by its German producer from its original 147 minutes to the current 105 minutes. With Kim Novak, Maria Schell, Sydne Rome, Curt Jurgens, David Hemmings and Marlene Dietrich, who performs the title number.
VHS: S09854. Currently out of print. May be available for rental in some video stores.
Laser: CLV. LD70268. $39.95.
David Hemmings, W. Germany, 1979, 105 mins.

The poet, novelist, graphic designer, film-maker and artist **Jean Cocteau** (1889-1963) was a leading figure in 20th-century French culture. Born in Maisons-Lafitte, Cocteau was educated at the Lycee Condorcet and Fenelon, in Paris. He first received recognition as a poet and soon emerged as a prominent figure within the Parisian avant-garde. Cocteau was prolific in a number of fields: in the '20s alone he wrote the libretto for Stravinsky's opera *Oedipus Rex*, the novels *Thomas l'Imposteur* and *Les Enfants Terribles* and the plays *Orphée* and *La Voix Humaine*.

In 1930 Cocteau made his first film, *Blood of a Poet*, which was financed by the Viscount Charles de Noailles (who also financed the production of Bunuel's *L'Age d'Or*). The film, which Cocteau described as a "poem on celluloid," was an effort to depict the inner life of a poet. Critic David Thomson asserts that *Blood of a Poet* "inaugurates Cocteau's overriding image of the poet passing through the mirror of dream...[which] is a very suggestive metaphor for the way a movie audience can pass into the celluloid domain."

During the '40s Cocteau wrote the screenplays for Marcel L'Herbier's *Comedie du Bonheur* (1942), Jean Delannoy's *The Eternal Return* (1943), Robert Bresson's *The Ladies of the Bois du Boulogne* (1945) and Pierre Billon's *Ruy Blas* (1947). He returned to directing in 1946 with *Beauty and the Beast*, a lyrical adaptation of the classic fairy tale. A year later, Cocteau followed up with *L'Aigle a Deux Tetes*, an adaptation of his own play.

In 1950, at the height of his film career, Cocteau produced his most significant work as a graphic artist. His final two films, *Orpheus* (1949) and *Testament of Orpheus* (1959), returned to the themes first explored in *Blood of a Poet*, extending his exploration of the myth of the poet as Orpheus.

Cocteau's influence cast a wide swath across European and American cinema. He was admired by French New Wave directors—particularly François Truffaut, who produced *Testament of Orpheus*—as well as American avant-garde filmmakers of the '60s. Summing up his film career, English film critic John Russell Taylor wrote that Cocteau "was the first artist of major importance in other media to accept the cinema as a medium of equal weight and importance, and the first to find his consummation and apotheosis in the cinema."

Jean Cocteau

Kamikaze Hearts

Juliet Bashore's dark, erotically disturbing lesbian drama boldly merges documentary and narrative storytelling in a revealing portrait of the lesbian underground. Sharon ("Mitch") Mitchell, an actress, and Tina ("Tigr") Mennett, a producer, are lovers and junkies. The film is set in a surreal, grim universe of two-bit hustlers and lurid sleaze. The women accentuate the intensely sexual nature of their relationship by making sexually explicit, pornographic films. "Only the camera, with verité charm, trembles during kisses here. This dramatic documentary...posits lesbian love as women's place of empowerment within an exaggerated patriarchal world—the real-life porn industry" (Alisa Solomon, *The Village Voice*).

VHS: S19104. $59.95.
Juliet Bashore, USA, 1991, 80 mins.

Kate Clinton: The Queen of Comedy

Kate Clinton and special guests serve up lesbian-themed comedy in this "Club Skirts & Girlbar Queens of Comedy Show." 52 mins.
VHS: S28567. $29.95.

Kiss of the Spider Woman

This is a visually hypnotic adaptation of Manuel Puig's novel about political and sexual repression. A flamboyant gay man, Molina (William Hurt), shares a cell with a militant revolutionary, Valentin (Raul Julia), in an unnamed Latin American state. Molina escapes the confinement and claustrophobia by recalling images from an obscure 1940s French film that serves as the film's title. The film is key to the curious predicament often faced by gay men who experience rejection from both sides of the political spectrum. Sonia Braga is the elegant performer of the film-within-a-film. With Jose Lewgoy and Milton Goncalves.

VHS: S00686. $14.98.
Hector Babenco, USA/Brazil, 1985, 119 mins.

Kizuna

In this first Japanese animated gay love story, Sam is a handsome, legendary high school fencing champion until his career is ended by a terrible car accident intended to kill his boyfriend, Enjolji, the son of an Osaka Mafia don. During Sam's recovery, their relationship intensifies but is later threatened by Enjolji's rival half-brother, Sagano, and his junior Mafia boss and substitute father. Based on the Japanese comic book sensation, this groundbreaking animated gay love story will thrill Japanese animation enthusiasts, foreign film buffs, and romantics of all persuasions. 30 minutes each. Dubbed in English.

VHS: S28504. $29.95. (Part I)
VHS: S28505. $29.95. (Part II)

The Krays

Peter Medak's stylish gangster drama about the rise and fall of the charismatic, ruthless twin brothers who dominated London's East End rackets in the '60s. One of the brothers prefers a "normal" existence, with wife and family; the other is a gay aesthete with a nervy sense of thrill and adventure. The dominant performance is supplied by Billie Whitelaw as their destructive mother. Cinematography by Alex Thomson. Screenplay by the painter, novelist and filmmaker Philip Ridley. With Gary Kemp, Martin Kemp and Susan Fleetwood.

VHS: S13828. $19.95.
Peter Medak, Great Britain, 1990, 119 mins.

Kamikaze Hearts

L

Labyrinth of Passion

Pedro Almodovar's second feature is a mock comic, sexual roundelay connected by the characters' incessant longing.

In a frenzied Madrid threatening to burst apart, the disenfranchised and repressed—transvestites, drug dealers, nymphomaniacs, incest survivors, disaffected punk rock musicians and Iranian fundamentalists—seek out danger, excitement and pleasure. With Antonio Banderas, Imanol Arias, Cecilia Roth, Helga Line, Marta Fernandez-Mura, Fernando Vivanco and Ruze Neiro. Spanish with English subtitles.

VHS: S12364. $79.95.
Pedro Almodovar, Spain, 1981, 100 mins.

La Cage aux Folles

Adapted from the play by Jean Poiret about a gay couple (Ugo Tognazzi and Michel Serrault) who operate a campy St. Tropez nightclub that specializes in female impersonators. They stage an elaborate plan to conceal their sexuality so that Tognazzi's son will marry into a socially prominent family. This is a peculiar, wild farce about shifting sexual identities and gender roles. With Benny Luke, Claire Maurier and Michel Galabru. French with English subtitles.

VHS: S00702. $19.95.
Laser: LD70756. $49.95.
Edouard Molinaro, France/Italy, 1978, 91 mins.

La Cage aux Folles II

Renato (Ugo Tognazzi) and his lover, the campy female impersonator Albin (Michel Serrault), operate a St. Tropez nightclub. Albin is upset by Renato's lack of attention and pulls out all the stops to maintain his sexual attractiveness. In the process, Albin unwittingly becomes involved in a web of espionage and international intrigue. With Michel Galabru, Paola Borboni and Benny Luke. English dubbed.

VHS: S00703. $19.98.
Edouard Molinaro, France, 1981, 99 mins.

La Cage aux Folles

La Cage aux Folles III: The Wedding

In the third installment, Albin (Michel Serrault), a flamboyant drag queen, and his lover Renato (Ugo Tognazzi) will inherit a vast sum if Albin marries and has a child within 18 months. With Michel Galabru and Benny Luke. English dubbed.

VHS: S00704. $19.95.

Georges Lautner, France, 1986, 88 mins.

La Cage aux Zombies

Writer, producer and director Kelly Hughes, author of *Blood, Sweat & Sequins* and creator of the popular public-access *Heart Attack Theatre*, achieved celluloid notoriety with this masterpiece of camp, which has been called "the *Naked Gun* of drag queen movies." When Norma (Cathy Roubal) and her lover, Brent (Eric Gladsjo), discover her gangster husband Lenny's (J.R. Clarke) drug money, the two run off with the loot to start a new life together. When Lenny shows up, the lovers, along with Tony the manicurist (William Love), make Lenny's life a real "drag" in this "towering inferno of blood, guts, and glamour." Stars Kitten Natividad of Russ Meyer fame and a soundtrack featuring the L'Orielles, Pansy Division, Scissor Girls, Kraaken, Homewreckers and Pussy Tourette.

VHS: S28515. $49.95.

Kelly Hughes, USA, 1995, 84 mins.

La Terra Trema

The first part of Luchino Visconti's never-completed trilogy about life in the economically devastated South of Italy tells the story of poor fishermen in the Sicilian village of Acitrezza who battle corrupt middlemen. "The importance of *La Terra Trema* as a work of art goes beyond the political aspects of the story itself: not only is the film shot on real locations, but all the roles are enacted by inhabitants of the village, who eloquently portray their lives for the camera" (Pacific Film Archive). Cinematography by G.R. Aldo. Narration by Visconti. Italian with English subtitles.

VHS: S03518. $89.95.
Luchino Visconti, Italy, 1947, 160 mins.

La Truite (The Trout)

American expatriate Joseph Losey's elegant drama about a complicated, ambitious woman (Isabelle Huppert) from the French countryside who relocates in Paris with her gay husband. With her intelligence and striking manner, she boldly defies tradition and privilege in her determination to advance within the business elite. Jean-Pierre Cassel is a prominent financier drawn to her intriguing combination of charm and tenacity. With Jacques Spiesser, Jeanne Moreau and Daniel Olbrychski. French with English subtitles.

VHS: S00714. Currently out of print. May be available for rental in some video stores.
Joseph Losey, France, 1982, 105 mins.

The Last Emperor

Bernardo Bertolucci's daunting meditation on Chinese history, culture, politics and life moves from the early 20th century to the aftermath of the Cultural Revolution. The story tells the dramatic life

La Cage aux Folles II

of Pu Yi, China's last emperor, who was coronated at age three and imprisoned in the vast spaces of the Forbidden City until he was a young man. Constructed in a series of elaborate flashbacks, the film covers Pu Yi's early tutorship, his hedonistic activities in Manchuria, the subsequent Japanese occupation and his political indoctrination and "re-education" following the Revolution. Like *The Conformist* and *1900*, Bertolucci is interested in the equation between sex and fascism; he focuses on a bisexual spy who seduces Pu Yi to extract information for the Japanese. Cinematography by Vittorio Storaro. Music by Ryuichi Sakamoto, David Byrne and Cong Su. Winner of eight Academy Awards. With John Lone, Joan Chen, Peter O'Toole, Ying Ruocheng, Victor Wong and Maggie Han.

VHS: S07372. Currently out of print. May be available for rental in some video stores.

Bernardo Bertolucci, Italy/Britain/China, 1987, 160 mins.

Last Exit to Brooklyn

Uli Edel's adaptation of Hubert Selby, Jr.'s stark novel is set in 1950s Brooklyn and centers on forlorn souls trapped in an unyielding, cruel universe. Two performers particularly stand out: Jennifer Jason Leigh as a tormented prostitute and Alexis Arquette as an innocent, tender transvestite. Stefan Czapsky's dazzling camera work and primal color schemes achieve a perfect synthesis of style and subject. With Burt Young, Peter Dobson, Ricki Lake and a brief cameo by author Hubert Selby, Jr.

VHS: S13289. $89.95.

Uli Edel, W. Germany/USA, 1989, 102 mins.

The Last of England

"Wrenchingly beautiful...the film is one of the few commanding works of personal cinema in the late '80s—a call to open our eyes to a world violated by greed and repression, to see what irrevocable damage has been wrought on city, countryside and soul, how our skies, our bodies, have turned poisonous" (J. Hoberman, *The Village Voice*). Derek Jarman's beautiful film synthesizes rock 'n' roll, Super-8, gay erotica and old home movies into a trenchant, aesthetically liberating study. Jarman "superimposes an incandescent Belfast over contemporary London.... The doomsday rubble landscape...is rendered with the imagistic panache of Kenneth Anger and pulverized a la Brakhage. *The Last of England* is sinister and gorgeous" (J. Hoberman). With Tilda Swinton, Gerrard McArthur, John Phillips and Gay Gaynor.

VHS: S09555. $29.95.

Derek Jarman, Great Britain, 1987, 87 mins.

Law of Desire

Pedro Almodovar's intoxicating study of the complicated relations between sex, politics and the church crystallized through a delirious three-way love affair. Pablo is a filmmaker who lives the high life in Madrid, engaged in casual drug use and homosexual affairs. His life is thrown completely out of balance with the arrival of his transsexual brother/sister, who becomes sexually entangled with the son of a politically prominent minister. "There's something to offend and delight everyone. Almodovar's sensuous style carries all before him. A life-affirming joy" (*Time Out*). With Eusebio Poncela, Carmen Maura, Antonio Banderas, Miguel Molina and Bibi Andersson. Spanish with English subtitles.

VHS: S06023. $79.95.
Pedro Almodovar, Spain, 1987, 105 mins.

Lawrence of Arabia

David Lean's finest achievement, *Lawrence of Arabia* is a breathtaking, historically expansive biography of British officer T.E. Lawrence that focuses on his stunning military and political victories in the Middle East. Lean uses time, space and character to build a complex, nuanced portrait of Lawrence. But the film romanticizes Lawrence without revealing much about his enigmatic personality, and, particularly, his homosexuality. Cinematography by Freddie Young. With Peter O'Toole, Alec Guinness, Anthony Quinn and Omar Sharif.

VHS: S17926. $34.95.
Laser: CAV. LD70413. $124.95.
Laser: CLV. LD70414. $69.95.
David Lean, Great Britain, 1962, 216 mins.

Les Biches

Claude Chabrol's elegant New Wave set piece charts the sinister sexual rhythms of a decadent ménage-a-trois. The story follows a wealthy woman (Stephane Audran) who seduces a young, elusive sidewalk artist (Jacqueline Sassard). They flee to Audran's villa in St. Tropez, where their relationship is disrupted by a charming, elusive architect (Jean-Louis Trintignant). Cinematography by Jean Rabier. Music by Pierre Jansen. French with English subtitles.

VHS: S16167. $24.95.
Claude Chabrol, France, 1968, 104 mins.

The Last Emperor   *The Last Emperor*

Lesbian Tongues

A revealing, fascinating and complex discourse on the private battles and personal joys of gender politics and gay sex. A wide range of interview subjects—intellectuals, artists, professionals and dairy farmers—talk about gay liberation, life, love and sex. With JoAnn Loulan, Joan Nestle, Barbara Grier, Jewelle L. Gomez, Lois Weaver and Deanie Williams.

VHS: S19265. $39.95.

Lesbionage

In this noir private-eye thriller with a sexual twist, two lesbian private detectives are propelled into a complex web of deceit, blackmail, kidnapping and corruption. The demands and pressures to solve the case place a tremendous burden on their personal relationship. With Lou Sullivan, Liz Prescott and Jewelle L. Gomez. 90 mins.

VHS: S19264. $39.95.

Joyce Compton, USA, 90 mins.

L'Homme Blesse (The Wounded Man)

Often compared to the work of Jean Genet, this film—which shocked the 1983 Cannes Film Festival—is the story of the sexual awakening of 18-year-old Henri, who has a violent encounter with a brutal man in a seedy train station. Henri then finds himself falling in love with an older man. "Absolutely amazing in its erotic power...a galvanizing psychological realism, sinisterly rendered by Renato Berta's icy blue photography, that has the outward grittiness of Italian neo-realist cinema with the more modern explicitness of Fassbinder" (Joel Weinberg, *New York Native*). Winner of the Cesar (French Oscar) for Best Screenplay. With Jean-Hughes Anglade, Vittorio Mezzogiorno and Roland Bertin. French with English subtitles.

VHS: S06588. $79.95.

Patrice Chereau, France, 1984, 90 mins.

Lianna

John Sayles' second feature is a provocative work on sexual politics and social persecution. The dissatisfied wife (Linda Griffiths) of a film professor acknowledges her homosexuality, begins to frequent the gay underground and initiates an intense relationship with a child psychologist. Sayles shows how Lianna's emerging sexuality leads to her isolation from her two children and her former community. "The love scenes are infused with a tender erotic glow that deepens the shadows around the titillation of *Personal Best*, and the comedy in Lianna's post-coital glee as she cruises for other women and announces herself as gay to people in laundrettes is irresistible" (*Time Out*). With Jane Hallaren, Jon DeVries, Jo Henderson and Maggie Renzi.

VHS: S00750. Currently out of print. May be available for rental in some video stores.
John Sayles, USA, 1983, 110 mins.

Liberace

From A & E comes this first authorized biography of the flamboyant Las Vegas showman who became the highest-paid and best-loved entertainer in the world. 50 mins.
VHS: S30108. $19.95.

Lifetime Commitment: A Portrait of Karen Thompson

Lifetime Commitment tells the sad story of Sharon Kowalski. She became the subject of a lengthy legal case of great importance regarding, among other issues, one's freedom of association. Kowalski was injured and then denied access to her lover Karen Thompson. As a result, Thompson has become a nationally recognized advocate of partnership rights for lesbian and gay couples. Produced by Kiki Zeldes and Susan Bruce. 33 mins.
VHS: S19454. $39.95.

Lilith

Adapted from J.R. Salamanca's novel, Robert Rossen's last film is set in an asylum. A handsome therapist (Warren Beatty) falls for a beautiful, emotionally unbalanced young woman, Lilith (Jean Seberg), after he discovers her in the embrace of an older woman (Anne Meacham). In retrospect, the film is even better than when first released. Eugene Schufftan's cinematography is lyrical, a succession of white-on-white compositions that is moody and haunting. "A remarkable attempt to dig a little deeper in an almost untilled field, and to throw some light on the relationship between madness and the creative imagination" (Tom Milne). With Peter Fonda, Kim Hunter, James Patterson and Gene Hackman.

VHS: S04662. $59.95.
Robert Rossen, USA, 1964, 114 mins.

Lily Tomlin 3-Pack

The Search for Signs of Intelligent Life in the Universe, Ernestine: Peak Experiences and *Appearing Nitely* are the comic standouts joined in this three-tape set. It brings Lily Tomlin's Tony Award-winning performances to video. 120 mins.

VHS: S27478. $59.95.

Liquid Sky

A deliriously kinetic mixture of high style, deadpan wit, tabloid fantasy and science fiction by the emigre Soviet director Slava Tsukerman. The warped story is about a lesbian punk rocker (Anne Carlisle) and her sexually curious friends, who are invaded and slowly exterminated by an alien parasite junkie who is searching for heroin or a chemical produced in the human brain during orgasm. Carlisle also plays the male lead, alternating between Marilyn Monroe and Johnny Rotten. "[Tsukerman's] aim of highlighting social malaise gets happily mislaid in a bizarre, often hilarious melee of weird drugs, weird sex and off-the-wall camp science fiction" (*Time Out*). With Paula E. Sheppard, Bob Brady, Susan Doukas and Elaine C. Grove.

VHS: S00758. Currently out of print. May be available for rental in some video stores.
Laser: LD71108. Currently out of print. May be available for rental in some video stores.
Slava Tsukerman, USA, 1983, 112 mins.

The Living End

Gregg Araki's breakthrough low-budget feature is a loose, stylish reworking of Godard's *Breathless*. The film is about two young men, a film critic and a narcissistic drifter, both of whom are HIV-positive; they undertake a mythic road journey after one of them kills a police officer. The film is notable for its electric, terse style and explicit, provocative sex scenes. A superb soundtrack of post-punk artists. With Mike Dytri, Craig Gilmore and Mark Finch.

VHS: S18692. $29.95.
Gregg Araki, USA, 1992, 93 mins.

London Kills Me

The first film by the brilliant novelist and screenwriter Hanif Kureishi (*My Beautiful Laundrette, Sammy and Rosie Get Laid*) is a darkly comic treatment of the London underground. The film charts the aimless wanderings of a renegade group of drug dealers who set up a squatters' camp. The movie's sweet, confused protagonist tries desperately to go straight after he's humiliated by a group of local hustlers. There's a vibrant sexual triangle played out among the three leads, along with a convincing evocation of atmosphere and local color. The talented American photographer Ed Lachman provided the cinematography.

VHS: S17968. Currently out of print. May be available for rental in some video stores.

Hanif Kureishi, Great Britain, 1991, 107 mins.

Longtime Companion

This powerful collaboration between playwright Craig Lucas (*Prelude to a Kiss*) and theater director Norman Rene is an emotionally devastating work that charts the impact of AIDS on a group of exuberant New Yorkers. The film moves between Manhattan and Fire Island, and begins in the early '80s with a *New York Times* article referring to the then-obscure disease. The film's concluding fantasy sequence is riveting. Bruce Davidson is superb as the group's leader as he confronts the absence of his companion. With Stephen Caffrey, Patrick Cassidy, Brian Cousins, John Dosett, Mark Lamos, Dermot Mulroney and Mary-Louise Parker.

VHS: S13301. $19.95.

Norman Rene, USA, 1990, 100 mins.

Looking for Langston

British filmmaker Isaac Julien's enigmatic and controversial biography of the brilliant, moody African-American writer and poet Langston Hughes. Julien interweaves the poetry of Essex Hemphill and Bruce Nugent with Hughes' prose, archival footage of the writer and period music to evoke the texture and rhythms of the Harlem Renaissance. A stylized, expressive piece of work about identity, sexuality, racism, repression and art, *Looking for Langston* is a cool, multifaceted portrait of a distinctive writer.

VHS: S16641. $39.95.

Isaac Julien, Great Britain, 1989, 65 mins.

Loot

Joe Orton's savage black comedy on English greed and propriety. Two petty criminals stage a daring bank robbery and stash the money in a coffin. Complications ensue when a string of unaccountable events prevents them from recovering the money. Sexual traffic between the criminals and other household members add even more permutations. Director Silvio Narizzano uses a complex narrative line, pace and tone to create a dizzying sense of off-center mayhem. With Lee Remick, Richard Attenborough, Roy Holder and Hywel Bennett.

VHS: S04438. Currently out of print. May be available for rental in some video stores.

Silvio Narizzano, Great Britain, 1970, 101 mins.

Los Placeres Ocultos (Hidden Pleasures)

A successful middle-aged banker leads a secret life searching out teenage prostitutes in Madrid's forgotten spaces. When he falls for a poor, handsome 18-year-old student, it has devastating consequences. Carefully crafted and well written, *Los Placeres Ocultos* was Spain's first explicitly gay film following Franco's death. Spanish with English subtitles.

VHS: S11636. $79.95.

Eloy de la Iglesia, Spain, 1977, 97 mins.

The Lost Language of the Cranes

A moody BBC adaptation of David Leavitt's novel about family secrets and sexual identity. The film centers on a young man's acknowledgement of his homosexuality and its volatile effects on the rest of the family. "Graced with subtle, intense performances" (*Time Magazine*). With Corey Parker, Brian Cox, Eileen Atkins and Angus MacFayden. Screenplay adaptation by Sean Mathias.

VHS: S18604. $19.98.

Nigel Finch, Great Britain, 1992, 84 mins.

Love Bites

This casual romp follows the adventures of a novice vampire hunter who falls into the lair of a gay West Hollywood Dracula. The film is a witty twist on the *Dracula* theme as the vampire hunter falls for the charm and sensuality of the 400-year-old Dracula. With Kevin Glover.

VHS: S11640. $29.95.

Marvin Jones, USA, 1988, 60 mins.

Love Meetings (Comizi d'Amore)

Pier Paolo Pasolini's uncharacteristic work is an investigation of sexual attitudes in Italy, highlighted by the remarks of author Alberto Moravia and psychologist Cesare Musatti. Pasolini is a trenchant interviewer who elicits his subjects' fears, obsessions and experiences with prostitution, homosexuality, marital relations and casual liaisons. Italian with English subtitles.
VHS: S12352. $29.95.
Pier Paolo Pasolini, Italy, 1964, 90 mins.

Love, Drugs and Violence

A collection of shorts encompassing comedy, experimental and music films notable for *Bust Up*, directed by Cathy Cook. In this experimental short, a female impersonator named Holly Brown puts on various psychotic characters over tea. Other (non-gay content) shorts on this tape are *A Trip to the Movies, 12 Pack, Purge, Slap, The Reagans Speak Out on Drugs, Violent, New Shoes, Ain't Gonna Pee in the Cup* and *Horror Brunch*. 60 mins.
VHS: S13837. $19.95.

Lust in the Dust

Paul Bartel's frenetic camp melodrama finds Tab Hunter and Divine among the collection of freak eccentrics who are caught in the desolate New Mexico landscape trying to locate buried treasure. All the while, Divine has dreams of finding her voice as a music hall singer. "Raunchy but irresistible. It would have made John Wayne lose his lunch" (*California Magazine*). With Lainie Kazan, Geoffrey Lewis, Henry Silva, Cesar Romero and Woody Strode.
VHS: S00785. $19.95.
Paul Bartel, USA, 1984, 85 mins.

Los Placeres Ocultos

The most talented and prolific German filmmaker of his generation, **Rainer Werner Fassbinder** (1946-1982) was born in the southwestern Bavarian town of Bad Worishofen. He attended secondary schools in Augsburg and Munich before studying acting at the Fridl-Leonhard Studio. After failing the entrance exam to the West Berlin Film and Television Academy, Fassbinder turned to writing plays and acting. He became involved in one of Munich's radical theater groups, the *action-theater*. After the police closed down the theater, Fassbinder formed his own experimental group, the *anti-theater*. Several members of the group formed an informal stock company of actors who collaborated with Fassbinder throughout his career.

Fassbinder's early films were influenced by French New Wave directors and American gangster dramas and B-movies. Like the theoretical cinema of Jean-Luc Godard and Jean-Marie Straub, Fassbinder's films were self-reflexive and sardonic. His most important formal influence was the German-born director Douglas Sirk, whose Hollywood films featured overwrought, melodramatic flourishes, set off by an ironic use of color, elegant widescreen framing and expressive decor.

Along with Werner Herzog, Wim Wenders, Alexander Kluge and Volker Schlondorff, Fassbinder emerged as a prominent voice in the New German Cinema of the late '60s and early '70s. His first critically recognized work was *The Merchant of Four Seasons* (1971). Fassbinder's *Ali: Fear Eats the Soul* won the international critics' prize at the 1974 Cannes Film Festival. In addition to his formal innovations, Fassbinder is notable for his identification with those outside the mainstream, and he was the first German director to prominently feature gays and lesbians.

Fassbinder employed a Brechtian approach to break down or counterpose traditional narrative forms. As critic David Wilson wrote, "Both formally and thematically [Fassbinder's] films often pivot on theatrical artifice: a recurring feature is the way physical and emotional stasis is abruptly shattered by an eruption of violence." With *The Marriage of Maria Braun* (1978), Fassbinder's films turned outward, as part of a historical examination of West Germany's postwar reconstruction.

One of Fassbinder's greatest achievements is his monumental adaptation of Alfred Döblin's *Berlin Alexanderplatz* (1980), a 13-part series made for German television. Fassbinder's final work, before his death from an overdose of sleeping pills and alcohol, was the posthumously released *Querelle* (1982), an adaptation of Jean Genet's novel.

Rainer Werner Fassbinder

# Macho Dancer

A brilliant film from the late Filipino master Lino Brocka that examines political and sexual repression. The title refers to a strip-tease artist in a homosexual club, a young man (Allan Paole)—coldly abandoned by his American lover—who befriends a street hustler and prostitute. After taking the job to support his family, he's drawn into a feverish and exotically charged milieu of straight and gay porno houses, nightclubs and sex shops. "Many of Brocka's themes are evident—an innocent being exploited in a wicked city, the difference between love and sex, male and female prostitution, police brutality" (*The Faber Companion to Foreign Films*). Cinematography by Joe Tutanes. With William Lorenzo, Daniel Fernando, Jaclyn Jose and Princess Punzaian. Tagalog with English subtitles.
VHS: S14597. $79.95.
Lino Brocka, Philippines, 1988, 136 mins.

Maedchen in Uniform

In this landmark film and adaptation of Christa Winslow's novel, an emotionally unsettled young woman (Hertha Thiele) is unable to adjust to the severe institutional order at a German boarding school. She gains comfort and subtle sexual assurances from a sensitive teacher (Dorothea Wieck). The forbidden relationship leads to dangerous long-term implications. "A powerful film with lesbian undertones which lend it a strange, subtle eroticism" (*The Faber Companion to Foreign Films*). Cinematography by Reimar Kuntze. With Emilia Unda and Hedwig Schlichter. German with English subtitles.
VHS: S02140. $24.95.
Leontine Sagan, Germany, 1931, 87 mins.

Making Love

This melodrama from Arthur Hiller (*Love Story*) features Michael Ontkean as a repressed homosexual doctor who decides to come out of the closet and admit his relationship with a sexually liberated writer (Harry Hamlin). Ontkean's eight-year marriage to Kate Jackson rapidly deteriorates into an emotional battleground. With Wendy Hiller, Nancy Olson, Arthur Hill and Terry Kiser.
VHS: S19448. $69.98.
Arthur Hiller, USA, 1982, 113 mins.

A Man Like Eva

This offbeat work features Eva Mattes playing the director Rainer Fassbinder as he swaggers, staggers, cries and bullies his cast and crew during the filming of *La Dame aux Camelias*. Eva, as the director is called here, "makes his mistress/leading lady undress and recite her lines while crawling, in order to get an effect he wants (humiliation). Later, when he learns the same actress has slept with an actor he's in love with, he delicately screams at her, 'Hasn't your cunt become hell?' in front of the entire cast" (Michael Musto, *The Village Voice*). Mattes gives a "stunning performance…a blood-curdling homage…." The film is "a hypnotic, unorthodox…paean to Fassbinder" (Vincent Canby). Cinematography by Horst Schier. With Liza Kreuzer, Werner Stocker, Charles Regnier and Carola Regnier. German with English subtitles.
VHS: S06589. $79.95.
Radu Gabrea, W. Germany, 1983, 92 mins.

Man of the Year

Dirk Shafer won the *Playgirl* Man of the Year Award because of his popularity as a nude male centerfold. Unfortunately, it meant he had to stay in the closet in order to reap the rewards of his position. This mockumentary follows the hilarious travails of the ultimate poseur.
VHS: S29857. $59.95.
Dirk Shafer, USA, 1995, 85 mins.

Macho Dancer

March on Washington: Part of the U.S.A.

The solemn Unfolding of the Quilt commemorating those who died of AIDS is the center piece of this visual and aural record of the March on Washington. Other moving scenes from the March include the memorial to the Unknown Soldier, the march through the streets of Washington, the Rally at the Supreme Court, and the spirit of togetherness at the Rally on the Mall. 30 mins.

VHS: S19453. Currently out of print. May be available for rental in some video stores.

Marquis

An audacious rendering of the political, social and sexual manners of the *ancien regime* and the class divisions and social tensions that produced the French Revolution. Adapted from the writings of the Marquis de Sade, Henri Xhonneux and Roland Topor's witty and vicious film uses elaborate puppets in human form to act out the erotic and sexual decadence. "Elegantly naughty with wry, intellectual satire. The film plays out all manner of human desire" (J. Hoberman).

VHS: S18104. $29.95.

Henri Xhonneux/Roland Topor, France, 1989, 89 mins.

The Marriage of Maria Braun

Rainer Werner Fassbinder's film is a kaleidoscopic interweaving of soap opera, comedy, history, politics and social satire. With her husband missing on the Russian front, Maria (Hanna Schygulla) achieves economic power and privilege through sexual and social cunning. When her husband unexpectedly returns, he is incarcerated for the murder of a black American soldier whom she comforted. Maria's romantic liaison with a wealthy industrialist (Ivan Desny) assures her power and prestige. The first of Fassbinder's loose trilogy about the West German "Economic Miracle" (with *Lola* and *Veronika Voss*). Cinematography by Michael Ballhaus. With Klaus Lowitsch and Gottfried John. German with English subtitles.

VHS: S01909. $29.95.

Rainer W. Fassbinder, W. Germany, 1979, 120 mins.

Matador

After the failed rape attempt of his instructor's girlfriend, a repressed, 21-year-old bullfighting student (Antonio Banderas) unwittingly confesses to a string of brutal murders of young men killed as if they were bulls done in by a matador. A feminist lawyer (Assumpta Serna) and the bullfighting instructor (Nacho Martinez) act as evil influences surrounding this naif with psychic powers. Even by Almodovar's peculiar standards, this is one of his most stylized, extreme works, grounded in '50s camp melodrama. "Surreal, iconoclastic and kinky, the film continues Almodovar's exploration into the link between violence and eroticism" (*The Faber Companion to Foreign Films*). Cinematography by Angel Luis Fernandez. With Eva Cobo and Bibi Anderssen. Spanish with English subtitles.
VHS: S10733. $79.95.
Pedro Almodovar, Spain, 1986, 115 mins.

Maurice

This Merchant/Ivory (*Howards End*) adaptation of E.M. Forster's novel explores the social and sexual hypocrisy of Edwardian England. Director James Ivory uses subtle tonal ranges to convey Forster's contempt for English propriety. The narrative concerns the shifting relationships among three men who are forced by social and legal codes to conceal their homosexuality. Set in 1910, Maurice (James Wilby) risks his standing and reputation by declaring his love for Durham (Hugh Grant), his Cambridge colleague who's trapped in a loveless marriage. The social drama, period decor and muted, understated photography (by Tony Pierce-Roberts) is beguiling. With Hugh Grant, Rupert Graves, Denholm Elliot and Ben Kingsley.
VHS: S06208. $19.98.
James Ivory, Great Britain, 1987, 140 mins.

Medea

Pier Paolo Pasolini reworks *Medea* using Freudian symbolism to construct a Marxist critique of sexual attraction, betrayal and revenge. Soprano Maria Callas achieves a mime-like fluidity and dramatic intensity as the tragic figure in Euripides' work. "Under Pasolini's direction, Callas becomes a fascinating cinematic presence, brilliantly brutal" (*The New York Times*). Cinematography by Ennio Guarnieri. With Giuseppe Gentile, Laurent Terzieff, Massimo Girotti and Margareth Clementi. Italian with English subtitles.
VHS: S00841. $49.95.
Pier Paolo Pasolini, Italy, 1970, 100 mins.

Meeting Magdalene

Marilyn Freeman's sexy short shows three women trapped in a love triangle overwrought with passion. Sarah is visiting her friend Jean in Olympia, but when Sarah meets Jean's lover, Magdalene, her friendly interests take a dramatic shift. 34 mins.
VHS: S27758. $24.95.

Men in Love

Following the death of his lover Victor, Steven honors a death bed promise to scatter the ashes in Hawaii. Unfortunately, the site turns out to be near the home of Robert, Victor's former lover, who is the guru to a unique male community. This leads to a cathartic reawakening of Steven's own sexuality. "Graphic yet romantic! Tasteful, never pornographic, yet fully physical" (*Bay Area Reporter*). With Doug Self, Joe Tolbe and Emerald Starr.
VHS: S14086. $39.95.
Marc Huestis, USA, 1990, 87 mins.

Ménage

This feverishly paced comedy from the talented French filmmaker Bertrand Blier (*Going Places*, *Too Beautiful for You*) is a brilliant sexual farce. The charismatic gay thief Bob (Gérard Depardieu) coolly insinuates himself into the troubled lives of Antoine (Michel Blanc) and Monique (Miou-Miou). The film is charged with Blier's characteristic wit, energy and sexual daring. "Blier is pitched somewhere between Luis Bunuel and David Lee Roth. He's a specialist in strident sexual slapstick" (J. Hoberman). Cinematography by Jean Penzer. With Michel Creton and Mylene Demongeot. French with English subtitles.
VHS: S16945. $89.95.
Bertrand Blier, France, 1986, 84 mins.

The Merchant of Four Seasons

The anonymous Hans Epp (Hans Hirschmuller) trades fruits and vegetables and enters a sad, desultory marriage. He finally drinks himself to oblivion. The film is a virtuoso balance of soap opera and social comedy and "Fassbinder's first film to gain general praise and recognition in Germany.... [It] is both bleak in its vision and enthralling in its presentation, and retains a sympathy for its hopeless chief protagonist" (*The Faber Companion to Foreign Films*). Cinematography by Dietrich Lohmann. With Irm Hermann, Hanna Schygulla and Kurt Raab. German with English subtitles.

VHS: S12467. $79.95.

Rainer W. Fassbinder, W. Germany, 1972, 88 mins.

Midnight Cowboy

British director John Schlesinger's landmark American film was the first X-rated movie to gain mainstream acceptance and Hollywood laurels. Schlesinger starkly explores the underside of the American dream gone awry. Jon Voight is Joe Buck, a lonely, confused Texan who performs sexual services for men and women. (The sequence in the movie balcony with Bob Balaban was revolutionary.) Dustin Hoffman plays Ratso Rizzo, a sleazy, small-time con who tries to survive New York's brutal streets. Written by Waldo Salt. Music by John Barry. With Sylvia Miles, John McGiver, Brenda Vaccaro and Bernard Hughes.

VHS: S01822. Currently out of print. May be available for rental in some video stores.

John Schlesinger, USA, 1969, 113 mins.

Midnight Dancers

Banned in the Philippines, this is the story of three young brothers who are trapped in the world of exotic dancing and prostitution which characterizes much of Manila's gay nighttime scene. Though they struggle along different paths, in the end, the violence of the streets brings them all to the brink of desperation. It is reminiscent of the work of Lino Brocka though more glossy. In Filipino with English subtitles.

VHS: S28048. $59.95.

Mel Chionglo, Philippines, 1995, 118 mins.

Milton Berle Invites You to a Night at La Cage

Berle wouldn't think twice about donning a dress for an easy laugh, so he's the natural host for this fascinating view of the tastes, ambitions and dreams of a group of female impersonators. The highlights are Gypsy, the gender-bending provocateur and host at the La Cage Revue, and Berle's hilarious take on Dolly Parton.

VHS: S04215. $29.95.

Milton Berle/Jim Gates, USA, 1986, 75 mins.

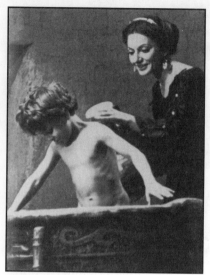

Medea

Midnight Cowboy

Mine Eyes Have Seen the Glory: The Women's Army Corps

Mariette Hartley, award-winning actress and the author of the best-selling autobiography *Breaking the Silence*, narrates this look at the Women's Army Corps. Known as WAC, the Corps was founded during World War II, paving the way for today's gender-integrated armed forces. Includes interviews with the former directors, officers and enlisted women of the WAC.

VHS: S27301. $29.95.

Dane Hansen, USA, 1996

Mishima: A Life in Four Chapters

Paul Schrader's visually complex dramatization of the life and death of Yukio Mishima, Japan's greatest postwar writer. His austere, rigid code of behavior seemed intensely at odds with his homosexuality. Schrader finds fascinating stylistic registers to shape the narrative, switching from deeply burnished and stylized colors to highly textured black-and-white footage. The film brilliantly mixes a mock documentary of Mishima's life with stylized recreations from his novels. Music by Philip Glass. Cinematography by John Bailey. With Ken Ogata. Narration by Roy Scheider. English and Japanese with English subtitles.

VHS: S00861. $79.95.

Paul Schrader, USA, 1985, 121 mins.

Mixed Blood

Paul Morrissey's apocalyptic vision of New York's notorious "Alphabet City" in the East Village is a cruel black comedy about ambition and class. Brazilian actress Marilia Pera plays a Brazilian warlord, a "drug queen" locked in a vicious fight with local drug runners over territory. It's a grim, deadpan vision of modern life, set off by its stylized violence and absurdist comedy. With Richard Ulacia, Linda Kerridge and Geraldine Smith.

VHS: S00864. Currently out of print. May be available for rental in some video stores.

Paul Morrissey, USA, 1985, 98 mins.

Moments: The Making of *Claire of the Moon*

A probing, behind-the-scenes documentary about the production history and personal difficulties in the making of *Claire of the Moon*, independent filmmaker Nicole Conn's highly personal and erotically charged lesbian drama.

VHS: S18773. $39.98.

Ellen J. Hansen, USA, 1992, 85 mins.

Monaco Forever

Set around the 1956 marriage of Grace Kelly and Prince Rainier, the narrative concerns the confusion set off by an enigmatic American who meets a mysterious French woman as they set off on a string of unusual and madcap romantic adventures. The debut film of Jean-Claude Van Damme, who plays the "homosexual." Cinematography by Daran Okada. With Charles Pitt, Martha Farris and Sidney Lassick.

VHS: S18917. $39.95.

William A. Levey, USA, 1983, 43 mins.

Mondo New York

This delirious, camp expose is an unflinching collection of vignettes, shot in 11 days, that surveys outlaw behavior on New York's Lower East Side. This freakish, uncensored travelogue chronicles the truly weird and bizarre; the filmmakers move inside cockfights, crack houses, S/M clubs and slam dances with an unabashed hedonism. The real stars are the engaging, terminally hip performance artists, musicians and street hookers who hold the fractured parts together. With Lydia Lunch, Dean Johnson and Ann Magnuson.

VHS: S04315. $14.95.

Harvey Keith, USA, 1988, 83 mins.

Mondo Trasho

John Waters' debut feature chronicles the pathetic final moments of an anonymous suburban woman (Mary Vivian Pearce). She is rubbed out when she is struck by a phallic-shaped Cadillac convertible driven by the monstrously cool Divine. The mayhem continues when Divine conceals the woman's death, moving her lifeless body through a disturbingly surreal vision of America. With David Lochary, Mink Stole and Mark Isherwood.

VHS: S05647. Currently out of print. May be available for rental in some video stores.

John Waters, USA, 1969, 95 mins.

Morocco

In her American debut, Marlene Dietrich plays an exotic cabaret singer who is stranded in Morocco. She slays every man in her path until she's torn between a wealthy French industrialist (Adolphe Menjou) and an attractive American French Foreign Legion soldier (Gary Cooper). Dietrich's brief hint of lesbianism, when she dresses in tails, is purely to wet Gary Cooper's appetite for her. "A cinematic pattern, brilliant, profuse, subtle and at almost every turn inventive" (Wilton A. Barrett). Cinematography by Lee Garmes. Written by Jules Furman. With Ullrich Haupt, Juliette Compton and Francis McDonald.

VHS: S02285. $14.98.

Josef von Sternberg, USA, 1930, 97 mins.

Mother Kusters Goes to Heaven

An average guy, a factory worker, goes beserk one day; he kills the boss's son and throws himself into the machinery. Upset by the media portrait that emerges of her husband and her exploitation by political opportunists, his widow is politicized and joins a revolutionary guerilla front. Fassbinder's ironic treatment of modern society is an indictment of anonymous industrialization and media duplicity. "Fassbinder's film is both a moving description of a woman's achievement of grace, and an excoriating description of a modern world—the world of hijackings, Patty Hearst, Watergate and Gary Gilmore—where it is often difficult to draw the line between journalism, show biz, crime and politics" (*Pacific Film Archive* program note). Cinematography by Michael Ballhaus. With Margit Carstensen, Karl-Heinz Bohm and Ingrid Caven. German with English subtitles.

VHS: S16695. $29.95.

Rainer W. Fassbinder, W. Germany, 1975, 108 mins.

The Mozart Brothers

A tortured Swedish opera director stages a highly unorthodox production of Mozart's *Don Giovanni*, destroying the stage to install a pool, removing the libretto and liberating the artists of their inhibitions. The conservative company's initial resistance is broken down by the intensity and passion of the director's vision. The film explores the unsettling, provocative nature of performance and art and the conflict between personal expression and the public's demands. With Etienne Glaser, Philip Zanden and Henry Bronett. Swedish with English subtitles.

VHS: S10930. $59.95.

Suzanne Osten, Sweden, 1985, 98 mins.

Mr. Wrong

Ellen DeGeneres, of the popular TV sitcom *Ellen*, plays a very unlikely bride-to-be in this outrageous comedy. Bill Pullman is the suitor who can't take a hint. Together the pair show how a relationship can deteriorate from a dream date to a nightmare. Joan Cusack, Dean Stockwell and Joan Plowright are also featured.

VHS: S29406. $19.95.

Laser: LD75816. $39.99.

Nick Castle, USA, 1996, 97 mins.

Multiple Maniacs

Loosely inspired by the Manson/Tate massacres, *Multiple Maniacs* is a bizarre meditation on white-trash aesthetics and an essay on camp and shock value. The fabulous Divine uses a grotesque traveling freak show as an elaborate cover to conceal her crime spree, as she robs and kills unsuspecting members of the audience. In the penultimate scene, Divine is raped by a 15-foot broiled lobster. With David Lochary, Mary Vivian Pearce, Edith Massey and Mink Stole.

VHS: S05648. Currently out of print. May be available for rental in some video stores.

John Waters, USA, 1970, 90 mins.

The Music Lovers

Ken Russell's highly stylized musical biography of Tchaikovsky paints a portrait of a tormented homosexual who conceals his sexual orientation in order to marry, though his extravagant repressions drive his wife into madness. Cinematography by Douglas Slocombe. Musical direction by André Previn. With Richard Chamberlain, Glenda Jackson, Christopher Gable and Max Adrian.

VHS: S14809. $19.99.
Ken Russell, Great Britain, 1970, 123 mins.

My Beautiful Laundrette

The exciting, brash and liberating British film by director Stephen Frears and novelist/filmmaker Hanif Kureishi has at its center the relationship between a Pakistani innocent (Saeed Jaffrey) and the leader (Daniel Day-Lewis) of a neo-Nazi movement in East London. Their playful and intricate gay relationship produces a series of revelations and insights. With Roshan Seth, Derrick Branche and Shirley Anne Field. Cinematography by Oliver Stapleton.

VHS: S02975. Currently out of print. May be available for rental in some video stores.
Stephen Frears, Great Britain, 1986, 97 mins.

My Father Is Coming

A German woman living in New York learns that her Bavarian father plans to visit her. On a moment's notice, she must pull off an elaborate facade of being married and successful. Her gay roommate poses as her husband but complications ensue when a string of bizarre circumstances result in her father becoming an underground sexual icon. She's drawn into a series of strange relationships with her Puerto Rican friend and a female-to-male transsexual. With Shelly Kastner, Alfred Edel and Annie Sprinkle. Cinematography by Elfi Mikesch.

VHS: S18412. $29.95.
Monika Treut, USA/Germany, 1991, 83 mins.

My Own Private Idaho

Gus Van Sant's daring revision of Shakespeare's *Henry IV* is refracted through the trappings of a contemporary road movie. River Phoenix is a gay narcoleptic street hustler trying to find his mother. His best friend (Keanu Reeves) is the bisexual, gilded son of Portland's mayor. Both are attracted to a Falstaffian rogue named Bob (filmmaker William Richert). In the middle sections, characters break into free verse and appropriate important passages from the *Henry* plays. Using Orson Welles' *Chimes at Midnight* as his model, Van Sant taps into the loose, fractured spaces of displaced dreams and people on the run. Cinematography by Eric Alan Edwards and John Campbell. With James Russo, Rodney Harvey and Chiara Caselli.

VHS: S15927. $19.95.
Gus Van Sant, USA, 1991, 102 mins.

The Mystery of Alexina

A startling work taken from a 19th-century story about Alexina (Vuillemin), a sheltered young woman who leaves the convent to teach at a small boarding school. Her strong attraction to the daughter of the school's owner unravels Alexina's sexual identity, leading to the startling revelation that she's a man. The balance of the film investigates psychological conflicts of sexuality and desire, identity and attraction. Based on the diaries of 19th-century hermaphrodite Herculine Barbin, which were edited by Michel Foucault. Cinematography by Bernard Zitzermann. With Valerie Stroh, Veronique Silver and Bernard Freyd. French with English subtitles.

VHS: S03955. Currently out of print. May be available for rental in some video stores.
Rene Feret, France, 1986, 84 mins.

My Own Private Idaho

Director, screenwriter, and producer **Todd Haynes** (b. 1961) has continually made stylistically innovative work which has amazed critics and audiences. Beginning with his short student films, evocatively titled *Sex Shop, Suicide* and *Assassins* (all made in 1983), Haynes explored controversial subject matter while pursuing a distinctive style. Educated at Brown University and Providence, he formed a friendship with Christine Vachon, herself a producer of important queer work (*Go Fish*), and together with Barry Ellsworth, they formed the film cooperative Apparatus Productions in 1987.

Haynes' status as an underground filmmaker was clinched with the release of *Superstar: The Karen Carpenter Story*, in 1987. This brief and unflattering account of the pop star Karen Carpenter used Barbie and Ken dolls along with music by the Carpenters to recreate the sterile, claustrophobic world of Southern California, Karen Carpenter's original home. This crossing of iconic figures, Barbie and pop stars, results in both a hilarious send-up of celebrity worship, and a serious investigation into the world which drove Carpenter to an untimely death from bulimia. A 1989 "cease and desist" court order forced future screenings of this film underground and assured Haynes of untold publicity. Humor, pop icons, the sterile southern California environment, and above all, illness and controversy, have been part of Haynes' work ever since.

Poison (1989) again brought these different elements together in three episodes. One is based on a Jean Genet novel; another is a spoof of 1950s-style sci-fi films and the third is a touching story about a typical suburban boy who becomes enchanted by an imaginary realm. Funded in part by a grant from the National Endowment for the Arts, this film received intense public scrutiny in the press. Significantly, it also won the 1991 Special Jury Prize Award in the Dramatic Competition at Sundance.

Safe (1995), Haynes' most recent film, stars Julianne Moore as a housewife in an affluent Southern California suburb who unaccountably becomes sick because of all the chemicals found in her highly artificial environment. Like Haynes' other works, this film explores illness and an isolating sense of otherness, issues which many critics find evocative of the status of gay men in the AIDS era. Undoubtedly this work touches on such concerns—concerns particularly noticeable in the sci-fi component of *Poison*, where a couple find themselves disfigured and outcast by a strange new illness. In light of these core concerns, Haynes' work has managed to cultivate a wide audience with themes particularly resonant for queer audiences.

Todd Haynes

The Naked Civil Servant

John Hurt delivers a commanding performance as the writer, actor and raconteur Quentin Crisp, whose monstrous wit was his greatest defense against the repression and social ostracism he encountered while growing up gay in England in the '30s and '40s. Adapted from Crisp's autobiography, the film is like its subject—funny, piercing and profound. Hurt's complicated, chameleon-like performance finds a grace and dignity.
VHS: S00914. $19.99.
Jack Gold, Great Britain, 1980, 80 mins.

Naked Lunch

David Cronenberg's daring reconfiguration of William S. Burroughs' text about heroin addiction, totalitarian political parties and sexual experimentation. Cronenberg grafts parts of Burroughs' life and writing to shards and fragments from the novel. Peter Weller is William Lee, a recovered addict and bug exterminator fleeing from his homosexuality. After accidentally killing his wife (Judy Davis), Lee evades the cops and enters the mysterious Interzone, where he encounters a bizarre group of expatriates, scientists, spies and writers. A terrifying investigation into a tortured writer's psyche, *Naked Lunch* is a profound meditation on the creative process. Cinematography by Peter Suschitzky. Music by Howard Shore, with original jazz solos by Ornette Coleman. With Ian Holm, Julian Sands and Roy Scheider.
VHS: S16382. $94.98.
Laser: LD71581. $39.98.
David Cronenberg, Canada, 1991, 117 mins.

Navajeros (Dulces Navajas)

An illiterate 16-year-old gang leader battles with police and rivals in the slums of Madrid in his quest for love and acceptance. From the director of *El Diputado* and *Colegas*. Spanish with English subtitles.
VHS: S03899. Currently out of print. May be available for rental in some video stores.
Eloy de la Iglesia, Spain, 1981, 100 mins.

Night of the Iguana

News from Home

Chantal Akerman's film connects avant-garde impressionism and narrative construction as part of her experiments with capturing real time. The film is a deft essay about European attitudes and myths about New York that visually contrasts the graft and squalor of the ghettos against the conformity and monotony of the suburbs. On the soundtrack a series of letters are read from a Belgian woman to her daughter. "Most simply described, the film is a portrait of Manhattan in which a generally static camera presents a succession of geometrically framed streetscapes—it's a spare and ravishing city symphony that takes its cues from Manhattan's own relentless grid" (J. Hoberman). Cinematography by Babette Mangolte. Narration by Akerman.
VHS: S13819. $24.95.
Chantal Akerman, France/Belgium, 1976, 90 mins.

Nice Girls Don't Do It:
Films By and About Women

This compilation of award-winning short films is a challenging, entertaining consideration of the lives, experiences and attitudes of women captured on film. The most provocative lesbian piece is *Nice Girls Don't Do It*, an explicit, raw look at female ejaculation. Other shorts in the collection include *Emergence of Eunice*, *You Take Care Now* and *Urban Steal*. USA, 90 mins.
VHS: S15541. $19.95.

The Night of the Iguana

Richard Burton plays an alcoholic, defrocked minister who, after being reduced to working as a travel courier for a Mexican bus tour, becomes preoccupied with three pathologically imbalanced women: a teenage nymphomaniac (*Lolita*'s Sue Lyon), a frustrated artist (Deborah Kerr) and an intemperate hotel owner (Ava Gardner). John Huston's sardonic wit and flair for camp melodrama sets the perfect tone and mood for this adaptation of Tennessee Williams' play. "This is a sharp, funny picture with a touch of poetry" (Leslie Halliwell). With Grayson Hall and Cyril Delevanti.
VHS: S04394. $19.98.
John Huston, USA, 1964, 125 mins.

The Nun

Night Zoo

A French-Canadian crime thriller that won 13 Genie (Canadian Oscar) Awards. Set in Montreal, Marcel, an ex-con, returns to the free world to find his father is dying, his girlfriend is a little crazy and a couple of crooked cops are after the money he has hidden away. The film begins with Marcel getting forcibly sodomized in prison. With Giles Maheu, Roger LeBal and Lynne Adams.

VHS: S07964. $19.95.

Jean-Claude Lauzon, Canada, 1987, 116 mins.

Nijinsky

Herbert Ross made this extravagant, visually flamboyant work about the tortured physical and emotional relationship between the brilliant dancer Nijinsky and the Ballet Russe impresario Sergei Diaghilev. It's a work about movement, pursuit and abandon, unsparing in its depiction of the jealousy and rejection Diaghilev felt following Nijinsky's marriage to a wealthy social patron, Romola de Pulsky. The film is visually set off by some astonishing ballet sequences. "The filmmakers never show ballet for its own sake, and have the courage to keep emotional dynamics in the forefront throughout" (*Time Out*). Written by Hugh Wheeler.

VHS: S09897. $14.95.

Herbert Ross, USA, 1986, 125 mins.

No Skin off My Ass

A young punk hairdresser meets an inhibited, baby-faced skinhead in a park, picks him up, and takes him home; they tentatively explore sexual roles. But the skinhead freaks out and goes back to his lesbian sister, who encourages him to go back to the hairdresser by saying, "Queers are smart, skinheads are stupid." Shot in non-sync sound, a tough, independent Canadian feature. With Bruce LaBruce, G.B. Jones and Klaus von Brucker.

VHS: S17751X. $39.95.

Bruce LaBruce, Canada, 1991, 73 mins.

Notes for an African Orestes

A daring film which follows Pasolini's travels through the African countryside in search of locations for his adaptation of Aeschylus' *Orestia*. The film's structure is distilled from the director's notes—it's diary-like. Pasolini imagines his interpretation—set in contemporary Africa—as a radical critique of Western imperialism. He also documents various local rituals in this rare, revealing look at an artist's creative process. "A key to an understanding of the particular Freudian-Marxist-Christian world view that was Pasolini's" (J. Hoberman). Italian with English subtitles.

VHS: S09928. Currently out of print. May be available for rental in some
  video stores.

Pier Paolo Pasolini, Italy, 1970, 75 mins.

The Nun (La Religieuse)

Jacques Rivette's long-banned, formally audacious adaptation of Diderot's controversial novel about social and sexual authoritarianism. Suzanne Simonin (Anna Karina), an impoverished young woman, is forced into a convent, where the extreme isolation and confinement heightens her emotional vulnerability. Rejecting the intense sexual advances of her Mother Superior, Suzanne escapes the convent with the help of a priest's intervention. The priest (Francisco Rabal) subsequently attempts to rape her, forcing Suzanne to flee into a violent, uncertain world. Rivette's long takes and complex use of somber, muted colors create a feeling of claustrophobia and despair. Cinematography by Alain Levent. With Liselotte Pulver, Micheline Presle and Christine Lenier. French with English subtitles.

VHS: S13606. $59.95.

Jacques Rivette, France, 1965, 140 mins.

Oedipus Rex

Pier Paolo Pasolini's interpretation of Sophocles' Greek tragedy. The adaptation is augmented with a modern prologue and epilogue. Pasolini uses the severe Moroccan landscape and brooding architecture to render a complex physical space. The ironic use of music (Mozart and ancient Japanese music) is masterly. "Visually, the movie is often astonishing, the harsh desert sunlight and dry buildings isolating the characters effectively" (*Time Out*). Pasolini said he tried "to make a kind of completely metaphoric, and therefore mythicized, autobiography; and second, to confront both the problem of psychoanalysis and the problem of the myth." Cinematography by Giuseppe Ruzzolini. With Franco Citti, Silvana Mangano, Carmelo Bene and Julian Beck. Italian with English subtitles.

VHS: S07333. $29.95.

Laser: Widescreen. LD71585. Currently out of print. May be available for rental in some video stores.

Pier Paolo Pasolini, Italy, 1967, 110 mins.

Old Habits Die Hard

A collection of short films by poets and filmmakers, arranged by poet John Giorno. The works include David Van Tieghem, John Sanborn and Mary Perillo in *Galaxy*; Coil in *Tainted Love*; Jim Jarmusch's *Coffee and Cigarettes*; Tom Waits' *Raindogs, Confetti, Clocks, Barber Shop, Evening Train*; Love and Rockets' *Mirror People*; Starr Sutherland's *Contact*; Diamanda Galas' *Double-Barreled Prayer*; Nick Zedd's *Whoregasm*; and Robert Longo and Megadeth's *Peace Sells*. Appearances by John Giorno, William S. Burroughs and The Butthole Surfers. 60 mins.

VHS: S11994. Currently out of print. May be available for rental in some video stores.

On Being Gay

Gay-rights author, lecturer and counselor Brian McNaught (*A Disturbed Peace*), who advises Boston mayor Ray Flynn on issues relevant to the gay and lesbian community, discusses the complications and feelings of being gay in a straight world. McNaught discusses the consequences of coming out, maintaining family relationships, establishing intimate relationships, dealing with religious concerns, and attaining self-acceptance. 86 mins.

VHS: S05994. $39.95.

On Common Ground

An idiosyncratic portrait of the tragedies and triumphs of the gay liberation movement. Writer and director Hugh Harrison uses a neighborhood bar as the communal setting to explore the feelings, passions, energy and excitement of gay liberation history, from the political urgency of the '60s to the alienation and social contradictions of the '90s. Cinematography by Ron Hamill.

VHS: S18245. $14.95.
Hugh Harrison, USA, 1992, 90 mins.

Orpheus

Jean Cocteau's film is a stunning meditation on life, art, sexuality and death. The poet Orpheus (Jean Marais) is infatuated with the Princess of Death (Maria Casares). Her avenging angel Heurtebise (Francois Perier) responds by seducing the poet's wife (Marie Dea), transporting

Orpheus

her to a strange, beguiling underworld. The movie captures "the poet caught between the worlds of the real and the imaginary" (*The Faber Companion to Foreign Films*). Cinematography by Nicolas Hayer. With Edouard Dermithe and Juliette Greco. French with English subtitles.

VHS: S00977. $29.95.
Jean Cocteau, France, 1950, 112 mins.

Ossessione

Luchino Visconti's remarkable debut film is freely adapted from American writer James M. Cain's pulp novel *The Postman Always Rings Twice*. Visconti transferred the action to the Italian countryside of Ferrara. The story concerns the torrid affair between an amoral drifter and the dissatisfied wife of a local innkeeper, who conspire to murder her husband. "Visconti transformed everything he touched— actors, houses, objects, light, dust—into symbolic elements of his personal lyricism" (J.G. Auriol). It is a film "which was to change the face of the Italian cinema and establish its world-wide influence" (Georges Sadoul). With Massimo Girotti, Clare Calamai, Juan

deLanda and Elio Marcuzzo. Written by Giuseppe De Santis and Angelo Pietrangeli. Italian with English subtitles.
VHS: S05922. $39.95.
Luchino Visconti, Italy, 1943, 135 mins.

Out for Laughs

An irreverent, anarchic collection of vignettes on lesbian and gay humor, sensibility and outlaw style in this hilarious send up of images, stereotypes and media representation. 30 mins.
VHS: S18916. $29.98.
Shan Carr, USA, 1992, 30 mins.

Out Takes

Ideas about gay sensibility, homophobia and gender roles on broadcast television are juxtaposed through scenes from two children's shows, *Pee-Wee's Playhouse* and a Japanese comedy. Rex Reed's extravagant critique of Pee-Wee Herman's program and first film underscores Hollywood's self-perpetuating closet and the threat posed by the show's subversive gay subtext. Reed's opposition to Pee-Wee is exacerbated by the performer's penchant for innuendo, double-entendre and gender switching.
VHS: S11638. $39.95.
John Goss, USA, 1989, 13 mins.

Out There

Three 50-minute tapes of loud, proud and outrageous standup comedy by some of today's funniest gay and lesbian comedians, as seen on the Comedy Channel. A portion of the roceeds from the sale of these videos is donated to GLAAD (*Gay & Lesbian Alliance Against Defamation*).

Out There

Hosted by comedienne Lea DeLaria. Performers include Suzanne Westenhoefer, Marga Gomez, PoMo AfroHomos, Steve Moore, Bob Smith, Mark Davis and folksinger Phranc. 50 mins.
VHS: S30435. $12.95.

Out There 2

Hosted by Amanda Bearse (*Married with Children*). Performers include Kate Clinton, Mark Davis, Elvira Kurt, Frank Maya, Scott Silverman and John McGivern. 50 mins.
VHS: S30502. $12.95.

Out There in Hollywood

Hosted by Scott Thompson (*The Larry Sanders Show, The Kids in the Hall*). Performers include Robin Greenspan, Jason Stewart, Sabrina Matthews, Shelly Mars, Rob Nash, Jackie Beat and Lea DeLaria. 50 mins.

VHS: S30503. $12.95.

The Outcasts

A brave film about three young homosexual boys who are ostracized by their families and community. Left to their own devices on the city streets, the boys are rescued by an aging photographer who provides food, shelter and a sense of belonging. Mandarin with English subtitles.

VHS: S05987. $49.95.

Yu Kan-Ping, Taiwan, 1986, 102 mins.

Outrageous

An offbeat, quirky comedy about the mutual attraction between a schizophrenic pregnant woman (Hollis McLaren) and a female impersonator (Craig Russell) who performs colorful, precise impersonations of Mae West, Barbra Streisand, Marlene Dietrich and Bette Midler. With Richert Easley, director Allan Moyle (*Pump Up the Volume*) and Helen Shaver.

VHS: S00983. Currently out of print. May be available for rental in some video stores.

Richard Benner, Canada, 1977, 98 mins.

Ossessione

Pandora's Box

P

G.W. Pabst's baroque interpretation of Frank Wedekind's play *Lulu* is an eerie depiction of erotic obsession and sexual abandon. The action moves between Berlin and London, as Lulu (Louise Brooks), a beautiful, charismatic chorus girl, orchestrates a succession of casual affairs until her fateful encounter with Jack the Ripper. "Louise Brooks...could move across the screen causing the work of art to be born by her mere presence" (Lotte Eisner). With Fritz Kortner, Franz Lederer and Carl Goetz. Silent with music track. English titles.

VHS: S00990. $24.95.

G.W. Pabst, Germany, 1928, 110 mins.

Paris Is Burning

Jennie Livingston's documentary delves into the radical subculture of Harlem drag balls to explore the intertwining issues of race, sex, class, identity and community among black and Latino men. These stylized, abstract performers congregate in "houses" and are prepared by "house mothers." The competition is driven by the contestants' ability to appropriate radically different characters and types (or "realness"), including schoolboys, business executives and military commanders. Cinematography by Paul Gibson. With drag performers Dorian Corey, Pepper Lebeija, Venus Xtravaganza, Octavia St. Laurent and Willi Ninja.

VHS: S16701. $19.98..

Jennie Livingston, USA, 1990, 71 mins.

Parting Glances

This authentic, understated work about the final 24 hours of a long-term relationship is a revealing and painful study of gay desire. The film is straightforward, honest and compelling, with neither artifice nor sentimentality; it's also a dark examination of the sexual coldness that has emerged with the outbreak of AIDS. Steve Buscemi is excellent as a musician ravaged by the disease. With John Bolger, Richard Ganoung and Adam Nathan. Directed by the late Bill Sherwood. Cinematography by Jacek Laskus.

VHS: S02016. $29.95.

Bill Sherwood, USA, 1986, 90 mins.

Paul Cadmus: Enfant Terrible at 80

A playful autobiographical portrait of Paul Cadmus, whose unconventional, eroticized paintings subverted established rules and norms in the '30s and '40s. Cadmus, while painting in his Connecticut studio, discusses his aesthetic influences and the personalities who shaped his work and art.
VHS: S02396. $39.95.
David Sutherland, USA, 1984, 64 mins.

Paul Cadmus

Pee-Wee's Collector's Gift Set

Eight volumes of the award-winning *Pee-Wee's Playhouse* 1986/87 television series are presented in this gift set. Episodes include "Open House," "Pee-Wee Catches a Cold," "I Remember Curtis," "Conky's Breakdown," "Store," "Playhouse in Outer Space," "Pajama Party," and "To Tell the Tooth." Stars Paul Reubens as Pee-Wee, Laurence Fishburne as Cowboy Curtis, and Phil Hartman as Captain Carl. 224 mins.
VHS: S28485. $99.92.

Pee-Wee's Playhouse Christmas Special

From the award-winning series *Pee-Wee's Playhouse* comes this Christmas special which features an all star-cast, including Magic Johnson, Cher, Whoopi Goldberg, Oprah Winfrey, Frankie Avalon, Annette Funicello, Charo, Grace Jones, k.d. lang, Little Richard, Joan Rivers, Dinah Shore and Zsa Zsa Gabor. 48 mins.
VHS: S28486. $12.95.
Laser: LD75988. $29.95.

Pepi, Luci, Bom and Other Girls on the Heap

Pedro Almodovar announced his stylistic preoccupations and thematic concerns with his first feature after a series of shorts on Super 8 and 16mm. This dark and raunchy film details the roots of Spanish exploitation films, sexual identity and role playing. Pepi, a wronged virgin, seeks revenge. As a result, Luci leaves her psychopathic husband for a lesbian affair with one of Pepi's friends. A motley collection of punks, transvestites and musicians round out this intriguing mix. Cinematography by Paco Femenia. With Carmen

Maura, Eva Siva, Alaska, Felix Rotaeta and Concha. Spanish with English subtitles.
VHS: S16918. $79.95.
Pedro Almodovar, Spain, 1980, 80 mins.

A Performance by Jack Smith

This is the only known recorded performance piece by the late artist/actor Jack Smith, made from an optically printed 8mm film original. Included are two works shot in Toronto in 1984: *Dance of the Sacred Application* and *Brassieres of Uranus*.
VHS: S27224. $59.95.
Midi Onodera, Canada, 1984

Personal Best

Robert Towne's beautiful, erotic film about the lesbian relationship of two world-class athletes, a shy, naive innocent (Mariel Hemingway) and a cynical, older veteran (Patrice Donnelly), who meet at the 1976 Olympic track and field trials. The complicated emotional rhythms are thrown off by the Svengali tactics of a dominating coach (Scott Glenn) whose demands for perfection undermine their relationship. Towne displays an anthropological insight into the rituals of the track milieu. With its slow-motion footage of grace, athleticism and form, the film is a profound celebration of the female body. Cinematography by Michael Chapman. With *Sports Illustrated* writer and former Olympic marathon runner Kenny Moore, Jim Moody and Larry Pennell.
VHS: S01013. $19.98.
Robert Towne, USA, 1982, 129 mins.

Peter's Friends

Kenneth Branagh's witty comedy uses the structure of John Sayles' *Return of the Secaucus 7* as six friends, members of an anarchic university theater collective, reunite for a ten-year anniversary over New Year's Eve at the inherited estate of Peter (Stephen Fry). During the weekend, they assess their personal and public successes, failures, family tragedies, heartbreaks and romantic and professional disappointments. Sharp performances from Branagh, Emma Thompson and Alphonsia Emmanuel. Cinematography by Roger Lanser. Screenplay by American comedienne Rita Rudner and her husband Martin Bergman.
VHS: S18725. $19.98.
Kenneth Branagh, Great Britain, 1992, 102 mins.

The Picture of Dorian Gray

A strange, unsettling adaptation of Oscar Wilde's haunting Faustian tale about a Victorian man (Hurd Hatfield) who enters a perverse bargain with the Devil (George Sanders) to retain his youth. As his work ages, he remains strong and vigorous, spared the vicissitudes of age. Cinematography by Harry Stradling. With Angela Lansbury, Peter Lawford and Donna Reed.

VHS: S01028. $19.98.
Laser: LD70656. $34.98.
Albert Lewin, USA, 1945, 110 mins.

Pigsty

Pasolini's allegorical film brilliantly interweaves two storylines. The first story is set in Medieval Europe, in which a cannibal wanders through the war-ravaged countryside devouring the weak. In the second story, a German youth, the son of an ex-Nazi industrialist, is more attracted to pigs than to his fiancee. "Pasolini ironically chronicles the 'existential anguish' of the children of the bourgeoisie" (*Time Out*). With Jean-Pierre Leaud, Ugo Tognazzi, Pierre Clementi and Anne Wiazemsky. Italian with English subtitles.

VHS: S18063. $29.95.
Pier Paolo Pasolini, Italy, 1969, 100 mins.

Pink Flamingos

John Waters' trashiest, most frequently reviled work is a vivid, stylized profile of mock-celebrity, self-delusion and American "competition." In Waters' monumental celebration of bad taste, the 300-pound transvestite surrogate Divine pulls out all the stops in her efforts to win the contest of World's Filthiest Person. The film is a succession of stylized scenes involving animal sacrifices, scatological extremes, lurid sex acts and, most spectacularly, consumption of dog excrement. With David Lochary, Mary Vivian Pearce, Mink Stole, Danny Mills and Cookie Mueller.

VHS: S05124. Currently out of print. May be available for rental in some
  video stores.
John Waters, USA, 1972, 95 mins.

Pixote

Hector Babenco's (*Kiss of the Spiderwoman*) breakthrough feature is set in the squalid slums of Sao Paolo. Its central character is the 10-year-old Pixote, who somehow survives reform school to find his way onto the streets and into drug dealing, prostitution and murder. The sheer power of *Pixote* derives from its unrelenting depiction of the brutalization of Brazil's street children who, according to some accounts, number three million. With Ramos da Silva, Jorge Juliao, Gilberto Moura and Marilia Pera. Portuguese with English subtitles.

VHS: S30982. $89.95.

Hector Babenco, Brazil, 1981, 127 mins.

The Picture of Dorian Gray

Poison

From the director of the notorious underground hit *Superstar: The Karen Carpenter Story*, Todd Haynes' audacious film tells three fluidly intercut stories of transgression and deviance. Each segment is related through different narrative forms and stylistic registers. *Hero* is a mock documentary about a seven-year-old boy who shoots his abusive father; *Horror* is a metaphor for AIDS shot in black and white, about a disfigured scientist who isolates the human sex drive; *Homo*, based on Jean Genet's *Miracle of the Rose*, is a searing account of prison life and sexual obsession. With Edith Meeks, Larry Maxwell, Susan Norman, Scott Renderer and James Lyons. Winner of the Grand Jury Prize at the 1991 Sundance Film Festival.

VHS: S15839. $19.98.

Todd Haynes, USA, 1991, 85 mins.

Polyester

John Waters' lurid satire of middle-class America features his longtime collaborator Divine as an abused housewife and mother liberated by a handsome drive-in entrepreneur played by Tab Hunter. The movie is notable for Waters' observations and sympathetic feel for outsiders and the dispossessed. With Edith Massey, Mary Garlington, Ken King, David Samson and Mink Stole.

VHS: S01046. $19.98.
John Waters, USA, 1981, 86 mins.

Portrait of Jason

Shirley Clarke (*The Connection, Cool World*) works out a multilayered perspective on race, sex and class. The loose narrative takes the form of a confessional. The film recounts the experiences of a middle-aged, articulate, witty, black, homosexual hustler (Jason Holliday).

VHS: S01570. Currently out of print. May be available for rental in some video stores.
Shirley Clarke, USA, 1967, 105 mins.

Positive (Positiv)

Rosa von Praunheim's film is a loud, angry call to arms in response to the widely-perceived government inactivity in fighting AIDS. Von Praunheim provides a forum for the militant actions of playwright Larry Kramer, musician Michael Callen and filmmaker Phil Zwickler. The film investigates the bold, aggressive tactics deployed by ACT-UP, Queer Nation and the Gay Men's Health Crisis to counteract public indifference. "Scorching, [*Positive*] is an inside history of the AIDS movement" (*The New York Times*).

VHS: S14152. $29.95.
Rosa von Praunheim, USA, 1991, 80 mins.

Powder

Sean Patrick Flanery stars in this allegory-like tale of an astonishingly pale young man with unusual powers. Though this oddly beautiful young man is taunted by classmates for his startling appearance, he forever transforms the lives of those around him in wholly unexpected and magical ways. With Jeff Goldblum and Mary Steenburgen.

VHS: S27604. $19.98.
Laser: LD75549. $39.99.
Victor Salva, USA, 1995, 112 mins.

Prick Up Your Ears

Stephen Frears' painful film about the class tensions, social repression and institutional hostility that characterized the turbulent relationship between playwright Joe Orton (Gary Oldman) and his lover Kenneth Halliwell (Alfred Molina) in 1960s England. Frears beautifully lays out the repressive political and social arena within English society. Alan Bennett's screenplay is adapted from John Lahr's biography. With Vanessa Redgrave, Wallace Shawn and Lindsay Duncan.

VHS: S06881. Currently out of print. May be available for rental in some
    video stores.
Laser: LD71278. Currently out of print. May be available for rental in some
    video stores.
Stephen Frears, Great Britain, 1987, 108 mins.

Privates on Parade

A frequently hilarious adaptation of English writer Peter Nichols' play about a gang of English performers, set in a campy revue in postwar Singapore. Denis Quilley is the aging queen and leader of an eclectic troupe that stages elaborate sketches for the "exotic" local community. The troupe is caught in a nasty crossfire between communist insurgents, government fascists and a covert gun-running operation. John Cleese is frightening as Quilley's straight nemesis, the company commander. With Nicola Pagett, Patrick Pearson and Michael Elphick.

VHS: S01063. Currently out of print. May be available for rental in some
    video stores.
Michael Blakemore, Great Britain, 1982, 100 mins.

Polyester

Sergei Paradjanov (1924-1990) was, with Andrei Tarkovsky, one of the leading figures of postwar Soviet cinema. Born into a poor Armenian family in Tbilisi, Georgia, Paradjanov studied music at the Kiev Conservatory and received formal training in filmmaking at the Moscow Film Institute. Also a self-taught artist, Paradjanov sought to reinvent the cinema, to find a new means of cinematic expression—one which linked other disciplines and creative forms. "We impoverish ourselves only by thinking in film categories. Therefore I constantly take up my paintbrush. Another system of thinking, different methods of perception and reflection of life are opened to me," Paradjanov said.

He served as an apprentice to Sergei Eisenstein in the '40s. Paradjanov's early works, which include five features, a film he co-directed and a short, are unknown in the West. His first internationally recognized film was *Shadows of Forgotten Ancestors* (1964). Critic Jonathan Rosenbaum described the film as "mystically pantheistic and lyrically exuberant...a mixture of paganism, ritual, poetry and dance driven by rapturous camera movements." A visually dazzling interpretation of a traditional folk tale, *Shadows of Forgotten Ancestors* examines an isolated community in the Carpathians, capturing in ethnographic detail the pageantry and spectacle of local customs.

Paradjanov's lyric style achieved its full expression in his next feature, *The Color of Pomegranates* (1969), a bravura work about the life, art and spiritual odyssey of the 18th-century Armenian poet Aruthin Sayadin (1712-1795). The film was completed in 1969, briefly shown in Moscow, taken out of the director's control and re-edited, and then banned for more than two years. A 16mm copy was smuggled into the West in 1977.

Paradjanov was repeatedly harassed and persecuted by Soviet authorities, who assailed his films for propagating "nationalist tendencies." In 1974 Paradjanov was arrested and charged with various "crimes," ranging from his homosexuality to trafficking in stolen icons. An international protest helped secure Paradjanov's early release from prison in 1977. He returned to filmmaking in 1984 with the poetic, mythical *Legend of Suram Fortress*, which was based on a Georgian legend. Paradjanov made only one other film, *Ashik Kerib* (1988), which he dedicated to Tarkovsky. Based on an *Arabian Nights* tale, *Ashik Kerib* is a sublime mosaic about the travails of a rejected suitor who endures a series of hardships to prove his worthiness.

Sergei Paradjanov

Querelle

Rainer Werner Fassbinder's 41st and final film is a manic adaptation of Jean Genet's 1947 novel *Querelle de Brest*. The story follows the sailor Querelle (Brad Davis), an unrepentant drug smuggler of extraordinary charm and grace. His growing sexual and criminal escapades attract the attention of a marine captain (Franco Nero), fellow criminals and the colorful denizens of a Brest brothel overseen by Jeanne Moreau. Even Querelle's brother is among those who are touched by this soulful but treacherous hunk. Cinematography by Xaver Schwarzenberger. With Laurent Malet, Hanno Poschl and Gunther Kaufmann.
VHS: S01080. $19.95.
Rainer W. Fassbinder, W. Germany, 1982, 105 mins.

The Question of Equality

Four documentaries, each one hour long, are collected in this video set about the growth of the lesbian and gay rights movement in the last 25 years. They include *Outrage 69*, *Culture Wars*, *Hollow Liberty* and *Generation Q*. Stonewall, the military ban and modern queer youth are just some of the issues covered.
VHS: S27705. $59.95.

The Color of Pomegranates

R

Rate It X

A subversive feminist documentary about pornography, or what the filmmakers call the "sexual landscape." Filmmakers Paula de Koenigsberg and Lucy Winer interview 15 men involved in the pornography industry. The interviews range from the cable television operator Crazy George to the publisher of *Hustler,* Larry Flynt, to a man who specializes in anatomically correct birthday cakes. The filmmakers paint a despairing picture of widespread chauvinism, in what they see as a wide-scale campaign to demean and objectify women and gays.

VHS: S05522. Currently out of print. May be available for rental in some video stores.

Paula de Koenigsberg/Lucy Winer, USA, 1985, 95 mins.

Rebels: Montgomery Clift

An in-depth portrait of Montgomery Clift which includes many interviews and long clips from his films, this documentary also deals extensively with Clift's homosexuality. Produced by Italian television.

VHS: Currently out of print. May be available for rental in some video stores.

Claudio Masenza, Italy, 1983, 90 mins.

Reflections in a Golden Eye

John Huston's interesting adaptation of Carson McCullers' novel centers around the homoerotic tensions that erupt at a Georgia military base camp. Marlon Brando plays a major who is inexorably drawn to a sullen private (Zorro David), a freethinker who has a penchant for riding nude on horseback. This unleashes a complicated vortex of adultery, betrayal and debauchery. (A disgruntled woman cuts off her nipples with garden shears.) Cinematography by Aldo Tonti. Music by Toshiro Mayuzumi. With Elizabeth Taylor, Brian Keith, Julie Harris and Brian Foster.

VHS: S04180. $19.98.

John Huston, USA, 1967, 108 mins.

Reflections: A Moment in Time

Xaviera declares in a lesbian correspondence magazine, "bright strong Scorpio looking for friendship." The open, daring message leads to her relationship with Megan, a terrified loner. Bridging each other's silence and isolation, they transcend the pain of racism and overcome

their fear of trust and commitment. "Classy erotica at its finest without crossing the line to pornography." "[The film contains] a love scene unrivaled since *Desert Hearts*" (*Bookwomon*). 30 mins.
VHS: S06366. $39.95.

The Ritz

Director Richard Lester (*A Hard Day's Night*) establishes a farcical, machine-gun pace in this loopy comedy about a pathetic mobster who eludes his demented brother-in-law by hiding in a gay New York bathhouse. Adapting his own play, Terrence McNally constructs a rogues' gallery of eccentric characters playing off hilarious sexual deceptions and mistaken identities. Music by Ken Thorne. With Jack Weston, Rita Moreno, Jerry Stiller, Treat Williams and F. Murray Abraham.
VHS: S01118. $19.98.
Laser: LD71475. $34.98.
Richard Lester, USA, 1976, 91 mins.

Rocco and His Brothers

Luchino Visconti's emotionally powerful return to his neorealistic convictions. After the Second World War, a peasant woman (Katina Paxinou) and her four sons leave behind the bleak living conditions of the South and settle in Milan. Structured in five parts, the film dissects the country's social, cultural and political framework through the experiences of five peasant brothers. It achieves a stark intensity in the brutal story line of Renato Salvatori as a sexually ambivalent boxer who destroys his brother (Spiros Focas) and his lover (Annie Giradot). Cinematography by Giuseppe Rotunno. Music by Nino Rota. With Alain Delon, Roger Hanin and Suzy Delair. Italian with English subtitles.
VHS: S07471. $79.95.
Laser: LD71306. Currently out of print. May be available for rental in some video stores.
Luchino Visconti, Italy, 1960, 180 mins.

Rocco and His Brothers   *Rocco and His Brothers*

The Rocky Horror Picture Show

A film that broke down the conventional relationship of an audience to a film, this lurid spectacle of sex and opulent decadence features a bland couple (Susan Sarandon and Barry Bostwick) who are trapped in a Transylvania mansion occupied by freaks, transvestites and the thoroughly peculiar Tim Curry. The transvestites steal the show. The musical numbers include the notorious "Time Warp," "Dammit Janet" and "Wild and Untamed Thing." With Richard O'Brien, Little Nell, Jonathan Adams and Meatloaf.

VHS: S14008. $19.98.
Jim Sharman, USA, 1975, 95 mins.

Romantic Englishwoman

Joseph Losey's witty study of middle-class British despair and social relations features Michael Caine as an uninspired novelist who is unnerved by his wife's (Glenda Jackson) private excursion on a weekend holiday. His fears are realized when she initiates an affair with a charismatic outsider (Helmut Berger). The social and sexual dynamics are shattered when Caine invites Berger into his home in a desperate attempt to rejuvenate his creativity. Writers Tom Stoppard and Thomas Wiseman adapted Wiseman's novel. Cinematography by Gerry Fischer. With Marcus Richardson, Kate Nelligan and Michel Lonsdale.

VHS: S01129. Currently out of print. May be available for rental in some video stores.
Joseph Losey, Great Britain, 1975, 116 mins.

Rope

Inspired by the Leopold and Loeb case, Alfred Hitchcock's daring formal exercise concerns two Nietzschean thrill-seekers who murder an acquaintance and orchestrate a pernicious game of pursuit and recognition. They invite their friends and colleagues and openly dare them to discover the corpse. James Stewart is the teacher who suspects something is dangerously amiss. Hitchcock composed a series of shots in ten-minute takes to establish a seamless pace and stasis. It was his first film in color. Adapted from Patrick Hamilton's play by Arthur Laurents. With John Dall, Farley Granger and Cedric Hardwicke.

VHS: S01133. $19.95.
Laser: LD70072. $34.95.
Alfred Hitchcock, USA, 1948, 81 mins.

Salmonberries

From the director of *Celeste* and *Bagdad Cafe*, German director Percy Adlon's political thriller with explicit gay subject matter concerns a repressed East German librarian who escapes her oppressive surroundings after her lover is killed trying to scale the Berlin Wall. Devastated and grief stricken, Roswitha (Rosel Zech, of *Veronika Voss*) travels to Alaska. Trapped in a grim, remote Eskimo outpost, she finds comfort and emotional fulfillment with a sexually ambivalent woman (singer k.d. lang, in her film debut).

VHS: S18844. $29.95.
Percy Adlon, Canada/W. Germany, 1991, 94 mins.

Salo: 120 Days of Sodom

Pier Paolo Pasolini's last film before he was brutally murdered is a chilling updating of the Marquis de Sade's novel, set in the final days of Mussolini's fascist state of Salo. *Salo* is an assault on the senses as Pasolini explores the outer boundaries of master/slave relationships and the roots of fascism. In a secluded villa, eight soldiers sexually and psychologically exploit a group of teenage boys and girls. "[The film] is alternately, surreal, harrowing, depressing, repulsive, and fascinating…a hellish journey through a sick soul" (*Faber Companion to the Foreign Film*). Banned in many countries (including the U.S., where it was seized by the Customs). Cinematography by Tonino Delli Colli. Music by Ennio Morricone. With Paolo Bonacelli, Giorgio Cataldi, Umberto Paolo Quintavalle and Caterina Boratto. Recommended for mature audiences only. Italian with English subtitles.

VHS: S11717. $89.95.
Pier Paolo Pasolini, Italy, 1975, 115 mins.

Salmonberries

Salome's Last Dance

British filmmaker Ken Russell's eccentric reworking of Oscar Wilde's flamboyant play is a postmodern pastiche of performance and outlaw sexuality, pitched between stylized fantasy and unrequited homosexual desire. Wilde is passionately attracted to a young aristocrat played by Douglas Hodge. While Wilde frequents a Victorian brothel, the owner stages a madcap variation of the title work, a long-banned effort starring a group of eccentric performers. With Glenda Jackson, Stratford Johns, Nicolas Grace and Imogen Millais-Scott.

VHS: S08232. Currently out of print. May be available for rental in some video stores.

Ken Russell, Great Britain, 1988, 90 mins.

Sammy and Rosie Get Laid

A subversive comedy, this film lampoons a colorful and bohemian London set. The lives of immigrants, radicals, punks and homosexuals are interwoven, offering a dazzling but dark view of Thatcherite Britain. Shashi Kapoor is the retired Indian political torturer who returns to England to visit son Sammy (Ayub Khan Dim) and daughter-in-law Rosie and finds them living in a war zone. From the director of *My Beautiful Laundrette*. With Claire Bloom, Frances Barber and Roland Gift.

VHS: S07290. $14.98.

Stephen Frears, Great Britain, 1987, 90 mins.

Scenes from the Class Struggle in Beverly Hills

Paul Bartel's caustic black comedy about social relations among the decadent, idle rich is a mock critique of American consumption and sexual gamesmanship. The servants of two neighboring aristocrats, a declining soap opera star (Jacqueline Bisset) and a nouveau-riche goddess (Mary Woronov), vow to sexually conquer their opposing employers. A monument to bad taste decor and shock lessons, the result is an intermingling of the surreal and the absurd. With Ray Sharkey, Robert Beltran, Wallace Shawn, Ed Begley, Jr. and Paul Mazursky. Screenplay by Bruce Wagner (*Wild Palms*).

VHS: S10994. $19.95.

Paul Bartel, USA, 1989, 103 mins.

Scrubbers

This is an edgy study about a young woman (Amanda York) sentenced to a British reform school. She has to summon her strength and cunning to survive the nightmarish setting, a cruel place populated by leather-clad, tough "girls" who fight over control of York's mind and body. With Chrissie Cotterill, Elizabeth Edmonds, Kate Ingram and Debbie Bishop.

VHS: S01169. Currently out of print. May be available for rental in some
    video stores.
Mai Zetterling, Great Britain, 1982, 93 mins.

Sebastiane

A truly unique film, shot in barracks-room Latin, *Sebastiane* is a tense, homoerotic rendering of the St. Sebastian legend. When a Roman soldier strenuously objects to the execution of a young Christian page, he is exiled to a remote desert outpost where he's tortured by his humiliated captain. Sebastian is played by Leonardo Treviglio, who spends most of the film tied to a stake, tormented by the sexual advances of the commander Severus (Barney Jones). The film's treatment of sexuality and political institutions provoked riots at the 1977 Locarno Film Festival. "*Sebastiane* has a pretension and a perversity about it that are surprisingly appealing in the long run. The very idea, you shriek to yourself, loving it the whole time..." (Rob Baker, New York's *SoHo News*). Music by Brian Eno. With Ken Hicks, Neil Kennedy and Richard Warwick. Latin with English subtitles.

VHS: S25523. $39.95.
Derek Jarman, Great Britain, 1977, 90 mins.

Seduction: The Cruel Woman

Wanda (Mechthild Grossmann) is a dominatrix and bondage specialist who services clients and stages elaborate sadomasochist rituals in this film. Mikesch's insinuating camera prowls and slithers, capturing the settings, stylized costumes and flamboyant dress of each encounter. In her private world, Wanda seeks out a succession of female companions, succumbing to the dark rages of desire and attraction. "This is S&M by Avedon, outfits by Dior" (Marcia Pally, *Film Comment*). With Sheila McLaughlin. German with English subtitles.

VHS: S12460. $29.95.
Elfi Mikesch/Monika Treut, W. Germany, 1985, 84 mins.

Shadows of Forgotten Ancestors

Senso

Luchino Visconti's luscious, operatic portrait of a decadent and corrupt aristocracy. Set in Venice in 1866, Alida Valli is a married Italian countess who falls for Franz (Farley Granger), an Austrian officer. When war breaks out, she is heavily divided over her patriotism, her outrage at his sexual betrayal and her obsession with the officer. A film of shifting moods and expressions, the story contrasts Livia's manipulation and treachery with Franz's passiveness and deceit. Cinematography by G.R. Aldo and Robert Krasker. With Massimo Girotti, Heinz Moog and Rina Morelli. Tennessee Williams and Paul Bowles worked on the limited English dialogue, which in some versions is in German. Italian with English subtitles.

VHS: S09353. $29.95.
Luchino Visconti, Italy, 1955, 115 mins.

The Servant

Playwright Harold Pinter scripted Joseph Losey's unsettling depiction of the strange activities of a corrupt manservant (Dirk Bogarde) who methodically causes the breakdown and dissolution of his ineffectual, ascetic employer (James Fox). "Losey is a subtle stylist whose major themes are the destructiveness of the erotic impulse and the corrupting nature of technocracy" (David Cook). Cinematography by Douglas Slocombe. Music by Johnny Dankworth. With Sarah Miles, Wendy Craig and Catherine Lacey.

VHS: S01180. Currently out of print. May be available for rental in some video stores.
Joseph Losey, Great Britain, 1963, 116 mins.

Shadey

A satire and thriller about the skills of Shadey (Antony Sher), an anonymous bureaucrat who is capable of converting visual images to film. Complications ensue when an assortment of strangers attempt to exploit his gifts for ill-gotten reasons. But Shadey has his own sordid agenda, securing a sex-change operation. With Patrick Macnee, Billie Whitelaw and Katharine Helmond.

VHS: S04768. $79.98.

Philip Saville, Great Britain, 1985, 106 mins.

Shadow of Angels (Schatten der Engel)

Rainer Werner Fassbinder collaborated with director Daniel Schmid on this film adaptation of Fassbinder's controversial play *The Garbage, The City and Death*. Much controversy surrounded one character in particular: a Jewish businessman (Klaus Lowitsch) who is always referred to as "the rich Jew." Ultimately, the story is more concerned with the outsider status of this businessman and the prostitute (Ingrid Caven) whom he hires to listen to him (and, on occasion, to perform in a mock wedding ceremony). Both find themselves out of place in a milieu dominated by prostitutes, pimps, corrupt policemen and perverse businessmen. Fassbinder appears as the prostitute's sadistic gay pimp. German with English subtitles.

VHS: S27664. $39.95.

Daniel Schmid, West Germany/Switzerland, 1976, 105 mins.

Shadows of Forgotten Ancestors

Sergei Paradjanov's masterpiece is a rich, dynamic tapestry of colors, movement, mysticism, ritual, symbolism and music, set in the remote Carpathian mountains. At the center of the narrative is the *Romeo and Juliet* theme of an impossible love between the son and the daughter of two warring families. The images are always startling, the camera moves incessantly; *Shadows of Forgotten Ancestors* is a work of true cinematic genius. Banned by the Soviet authorities. The "film confirmed that Paradjanov was 'dangerous' because he was committed to artifice—and imagination" (*Time Out*). Cinematography by Viktor Bestayeva. Music by Y. Shorik. With Ivan Nikolaychuk, Larisa Kadochiniklova and Tatiana Bestayeva. Ukranian with English subtitles.

VHS: S07576. $29.95.

Sergei Paradjanov, USSR, 1964, 99 mins.

She Must Be Seeing Things

New York independent director Sheila McLaughlin directs this tender, emotionally resonant film about the difficult connections between a lesbian couple. Agatha is a firmly independent international lawyer and Jo is an expressive and carefree filmmaker. Jo surreptitiously reads Agatha's private diary and is provoked into fits of mad jealousy and bizarre behavior, secretly dressing in drag to shadow her coy lover. The film is "groundbreaking in its understated portrayal of sophisticated urban lesbians exploring such dynamics as sex and sexuality, career and commitment, fidelity and companionship. The film gives us characters who are richly realistic and demonstrates that McLaughlin is a complex and refreshingly thoughtful talent" (*New York Native*). With Sheila Dabney and Lois Weaver.

VHS: S10941. $29.95.

Sheila McLaughlin, USA, 1988, 85 mins.

Short Eyes

Robert M. Young's grimly naturalistic, abrasive adaptation of Miguel Pinero's play about social confinement, sexual fear and the Darwinian struggle for survival of the men locked up in a brutal New York prison. The title *Short Eyes* refers to a child abuser played by Bruce Davison. With Jose Perez, Nathan George, Don Blakely and Shawn Elliott.

VHS: S01196. Currently out of print. May be available for rental in some video stores.

Robert M. Young, USA, 1977, 104 mins.

Silence

This film is a part of Ingmar Bergman's trilogy dealing with the existence of God. Ingrid Thulin and Gunnel Lindblom are stranded in

She Must Be Seeing Things

a remote village where the language is incomprehensible. Bergman openly portrays Thulin's latent desire for her sister, and Lindblom's compulsive sexuality. With Jorgen Lindstrom and Hakan Jahnberg. Swedish with English subtitles.

VHS: S02773. $24.95.
Ingmar Bergman, Sweden, 1963, 96 mins.

Silent Pioneers

Senior members of lesbian and gay communities share their memories about gay life in this documentary. Sometimes tragic and sometimes funny, their recollections are always personal and poignant. This film offers a unique view of an era less tolerant of sexual minorities.

VHS: S27614. $39.95.
Lucy Winer, USA, 1985, 54 mins.

Silence = Death

Rosa von Praunheim's vital historical document explores the rage and vivid, angry responses of New York artists to the devastating consequences of AIDS within the gay community. The documentary is an impressionistic call to arms, as a series of artists—David Wojnarowicz, Rafael Gamba, Keith Haring and poet Allen Ginsberg—use their skills of persuasion and artistry to heighten AIDS awareness through music, film, art, theater, literature and dance. "Uncompromising, political, graphic looks from the inside. It's easy to get caught up in the passion of the subject" (*New York Newsday*).

VHS: S14148. $29.95.
Rosa von Praunheim, USA, 1991, 60 mins.

Silkwood

Mike Nichols' powerful work on the controversial life and mysterious death of Karen Silkwood (Meryl Streep), who reported hazardous working conditions at the Oklahoma Kerr-McGhee nuclear plant. The evening she was to meet a *New York Times* reporter, she was killed in a single-car accident. Written by Nora Ephron and Alice Arlen, the film is notable for a beautifully realized triangle between Silkwood, her lover (Kurt Russell) and their roommate (Cher). Cher plays a lesbian who carries out a funny, tender relationship with a local beautician (Diana Scarwid). With Craig T. Nelson, Fred Ward, Ron Silver, Charles Hallahan and David Strathairn.

VHS: S01202. $19.95.
Mike Nichols, USA, 1983, 128 mins.

Since Stonewall

Ten diverse, short films from the '70s, '80s and early '90s that contrast the feelings, fears, humor, artistry and changing realities of the personal and professional consequences of being gay in America. The highlight of the program is *Discipline of DE*, a short film by Gus Van Sant, based on a short story by William S. Burroughs. The other films include *Which Is Scary, Queerdom, AIDSCREAM, Song from an Angel, Triangle, Anton, Bust Up, "976-"* and *Final Solutions*. USA, 80 mins. VHS: S15542. $19.95.

Siren

Shot on location in London, this erotic lesbian film has all the makings of a delightful fantasy. Ella is captivated by Jodie, a writer of erotic fiction. At Jodie's lavish estate, titillation and more await this young and sexy couple.
VHS: S27448. $29.95.
Sarah Swords, USA/Great Britain, 1996, 45 mins.

Sotto, Sotto

Lina Wertmuller's sexual farce about an insanely jealous husband who comes unglued after his wife declares that she's in love with someone else. The husband undertakes an odyssey to track down his wife's lover, not realizing the suspect is his wife's best friend, Adele. With Enrico Montesano, Veronica Lario, Luisa de Santis and Massimo Wertmuller. Italian with English subtitles.
VHS: S01234. $19.95.
Lina Wertmuller, Italy, 1984, 104 mins.

Spartacus

Stanley Kubrick's final American film is an epic about heroism in conflict with social and political oppression. Kirk Douglas leads a violent slave rebellion against the Roman Empire. Written by blacklisted author Dalton Trumbo, the film focuses on the battle of wills between slave and captor. The 196-minute restored version features a gay seduction of slave Tony Curtis by decadent Roman officer Laurence Olivier (whose voice had to be electronically duplicated by Anthony Hopkins). Cinematography by Russell Metty. With Jean Simmons, Charles Laughton, Peter Ustinov, John Gavin and Nina Foch.
VHS: S15075. $19.95.
Stanley Kubrick, USA, 1960, 196 mins.

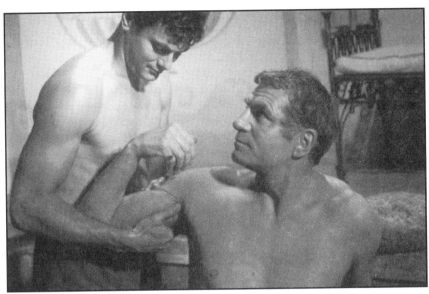
Spartacus

A Special Day

Ettore Scola's heartbreaking pastoral about two indistinct loners, a dissatisfied housewife (Sophia Loren) and an unsettled homosexual radio journalist (Marcello Mastroianni). They begin to develop a fast, enduring friendship on the afternoon of Hitler's visit to Mussolini's Rome. Scola beautifully plays off their casual deceptions. Cinematography by Pasqualino De Santis. With John Vernon, Francoise Berd and Nicole Magny. English dubbed.

VHS: S01237. Currently out of print. May be available for rental in some video stores.

Laser: LD71335. Currently out of print. May be available for rental in some video stores.

Ettore Scola, Italy, 1977, 110 mins.

Spetters

Dutch filmmaker Paul Verhoeven uses a motorcross championship to explore the homoerotic tensions of three young men, each obsessed with a beautiful, enigmatic hot dog stand owner. Verhoeven combines high melodrama with explicit sex sequences and a gloriously romantic visual style. Cinematography by Jost Vacano. With Tom Scherpenzeel, Kaya, Toon Agterberg and Maarten Spanjer. Cameo appearance by Rutger Hauer. Dutch with English subtitles.

VHS: S18627. $39.95.

Paul Verhoeven, Holland, 1983, 109 mins.

Spike of Bensonhurst

Paul Morrissey's colorful, raw Brooklyn village comedy concerns a cocky young boxer (Sasha Mitchell) who dreams of getting a shot at the brass ring. His dream is interrupted when he antagonizes the neighborhood gangsters—by romancing the don's daughter—who control the local fight circuit. This film is a gritty, unsavory depiction of the world of professional boxing. Some eccentric off-center characters, including Geraldine Smith's caustic portrayal of Mitchell's lesbian mother, lend resonance and spark. With Ernest Borgnine, Anne DeSalvo, Sylvia Miles and Talisa Soto.

VHS: S08508. Currently out of print. May be available for rent in some video stores.

Paul Morrissey, USA, 1988, 101 mins.

The Stationmaster's Wife

Set during the Weimar Republic, Fassbinder brilliantly evokes the desperation and despair of postwar Germany as realized in the heartbreak and unhappiness of the wife of a provincial stationmaster. Elisabeth Trissenaar is the bored wife who engages in a series of flamboyant affairs. Her pleasant, attentive husband (Kurt Raab) is no match for the succession of oppressive lovers to whom she falls prey. Fassbinder dramatizes the sexual and political tensions through a highly stylized, Sirkian use of ironic colors, melodrama and tight framing. Cinematography by Michael Ballhaus. With Bernhard Helfrich, Karl-Heinz von Hassel and Udo Kier. German with English subtitles.

VHS: S18933. $79.95.

Rainer W. Fassbinder, W. Germany, 1977, 113 mins.

Steaming

The final film of American expatriate Joseph Losey is an adaptation of Nell Dunn's play about the political and sexual attitudes among six independent women who gather at a decaying London bathhouse. Freed from a suffocating patriarchy and strict gender roles, the women break down and reveal intimate secrets in a palpable search for recognition. With Vanessa Redgrave, Sarah Miles, Diana Dors and Patti Love.

VHS: S02776. $19.95.

Joseph Losey, Great Britain, 1984, 102 mins.

Stiff Sheets

A colorful, impressionistic documentary about an agitprop/drag fashion show presented by a collective of gay artists who staged a seven-day, round-the-clock vigil at County/USC Medical Center in Los Angeles to protest the appalling lack of AIDS services, the public's indifference and the acute absence of facilities in Los Angeles-area hospitals.

VHS: S11637. $39.95.
John Goss, USA, 1989, 19 mins.

Straight for the Heart

Lea Pool's dazzling erotic feature centers on a cynical photojournalist who returns to Montreal and becomes involved in a bisexual triangle. After he's simultaneously abandoned by both lovers, he embarks on a dangerous inner voyage in which he compensates for his loneliness and despair by photographing the streets, architecture and textures of Montreal. He eventually falls into a tentative friendship with Quentin, a deaf window washer. "A film filled with visual poetry, a compelling drama [that's] stunningly filmed" (*The New York Times*). Winner of the 1988 Canadian Genie Award.

VHS: S18408. $39.95.
Lea Pool, Canada, 1988, 92 mins.

Strange Fruit

This compilation of works poses questions in regard to the struggle of women, black women, homosexuality, black homosexuality and the nude. Thematically bound to Billie Holiday's "Strange Fruit," this presentation seeks to inspect and inspire "difference" through the lens of identity politics. Artists and films featured: Chad Carter, *Ataxiaflagris*; Lisa Austin, *Breaking Ground*; George Kuchar, *Indian Summer*; Yvain Reid/Reginald Cox, *Passage*; Rodney O'Neal Austin, *Pop Tarts Come in One Size*; Holly Purdue, *Behind the Door*; Karla Milosevich, *Drive Me Under*; Veronica Klaus, *How Long Must I Wait for You?*; Georgia Wright, *Kachapati*; and Cauleen Smith, *Chronicles of a Lying Spirit*. 59 mins.

VHS: S30003. $49.95.

Streamers

Robert Altman's taut adaptation of David Rabe's play about the sexual, political and racial tensions among four Army recruits on the eve of their induction in Vietnam. The movie unleashes the tension between masculinity and race and explores how gay sexuality threatens the established order. "Confusion and confinement are the keynotes here: freedom of thought and action has been removed from these boys, with the result that finally they turn with inexorable anguish upon one another. Altman allows the cast plenty of opportunity to excel with spontaneous, vivid performances, subtly explored through a hesitantly prowling camera" (*Time Out*). With Matthew Modine, Michael Wright, Mitchell Lichtenstein and George Dzundza.

VHS: S01267. $29.95.
Robert Altman, USA, 1983, 118 mins.

A Streetcar Named Desire

In Elia Kazan's gothic treatment of Tennessee Williams' play, Blanche du Bois (the brooding Vivien Leigh) is a fading descendant of the once prominent Southern aristocracy, who gets entangled in the lives of her plain, direct sister (Kim Hunter) and her brutal, animalistic husband, Stanley Kowalski (Marlon Brando). The action unfolds in the rhythms and seamy underside of New Orleans' French Quarter. "Kazan achieves a sort of theatrical intensity in which the sweaty realism sometimes clashes awkwardly with the stylization that heightens the dialogue into a kind of poetry" (*Time Out*). Cinematography by Harry Stradling. Score by Alex North. With Karl Malden and Randy Bond.

VHS: S21085. $19.95.
Laser: LD70687. $39.98.
Elia Kazan, USA, 1951, 122 mins.

A Streetcar Named Desire

Jessica Lange is Blanche DuBois to Alec Baldwin's Stanley Kowalski, in this full, uncut film version of Tennessee Williams' immortal play. Lange won a Golden Globe for her portrayal of the delicate and mad woman, who relies "on the kindness of strangers." John Goodman and Diane Lane also star.

VHS: S27744. $79.95.
Glenn Jordan, USA, 1995, 156 mins.

Suddenly, Last Summer

Tennessee Williams' one-act play is expanded into a work about psychological trauma, sexual exploitation and cannibalism. In Gore Vidal's adaptation, a fragile young woman (Elizabeth Taylor) goes mad after she witnesses the brutal killing of her cousin, a gay poet. Katharine Hepburn plays a sinister matriarch who tries to manipulate a young surgeon (Montgomery Clift) into performing a lobotomy to erase Taylor's mental duress. Cinematography by Jack Hildyard. Music by Buxton Orr and Malcolm Arnold. With Albert Dekker, Mercedes McCambridge and Gary Raymond.

VHS: S01277. $19.95.
Joseph L. Mankiewicz, USA, 1959, 114 mins.

Summer Vacation: 1999

Four boys experience the confusion and pain of romantic love, sexual awareness and jealousy in this beautifully realized film. Left behind at boarding school during their summer vacation, their idyll is disrupted by the arrival of a mysterious youth with an eerie resemblance to a dead friend. Director Shusuke Kaneko creates haunting imagery of youth suspended between innocence and experience, androgyny and sexual maturity. With Eri Miyagima, Miyki Nakano, Tomoko Otakra and Rie Mizuhara. Japanese with English subtitles.

VHS: S13917. $69.95.
Shusuke Kaneko, Japan, 1988, 90 mins.

Sunday Bloody Sunday

John Schlesinger's film dramatizes a complicated three-way love affair. A sexually ambivalent designer (Peter Finch) balances his precarious emotional relationship with a callous doctor (Murray Head) and a female executive (Glenda Jackson). "Scene by scene, [the film] is both adult and absorbing, with an overpowering mass of sociological detail about the way we live" (Leslie Halliwell). Screenplay by the late *New Yorker* film critic and short story writer Penelope Gilliatt. Cinematography by Billy Williams. With Peggy Ashcroft, Maurice Denham and Vivian Pickles.

VHS: 01283. $19.95.
Laser: LD71182. $49.95.
John Schlesinger, Great Britain, 1971, 110 mins.

Superstar: The Life and Times of Andy Warhol

Chuck Workman's documentary offers a fascinating assessment of the rise and fall of the seminal pop artist and filmmaker Andy Warhol. The film deconstructs the Warhol iconography, offering revealing anecdotes and stories from family members, former lovers, artistic collaborators and rivals. Moving from the sublime (the nature of his art) to the absurd (his appearance on *The Love Boat*), *Superstar* is an engaging work that penetrates the grace and dignity of the man behind the artifice. The film includes interviews with Dennis Hopper, Tom Wolfe, Sylvia Miles and David Hockney.

VHS: S15135. $14.98.
Chuck Workman, USA, 1990. 88 mins.

Swoon

Tom Kalin's feature debut is an unorthodox reconsideration of the Leopold and Loeb case, in which two University of Chicago intellectuals attempt the "perfect" crime—the kidnapping of a 12-year-old boy which results in his death. This assured, suggestive work provides a historical and sexual context for the crime: Kalin argues the crime's roots sprang from a deep and unapologetic homoerotic fixation. Cinematography by Ellen Kuras. With Daniel Schlachet, Michael Kirby, Craig Chester and Ron Vawter.

VHS: S18518. $19.95.
Tom Kalin, USA, 1992, 91 mins.

Swoon

The poet, theorist, filmmaker and essayist **Pier Paolo Pasolini** (1922-75) was born in Bologna the year Mussolini attained power. He was educated at the secondary school Reggio Emilia de Galvani and the University of Bologna. He wrote in his native Friuli dialect and was instrumental in popularizing regional poetry. Pasolini achieved early prominence as a poet, publishing his first works when he was 20. He also contributed to the important theoretical journal *Corriere di Lugano*. He was drafted into the army and captured by German forces following Italy's surrender in 1943. He later escaped.

Pasolini was a highly accomplished Renaissance man, a novelist, an essayist and a brilliant social, literary and political theorist. He was an incisive thinker who possessed an endlessly curious mind. His writings, ruminations on the nature of individualism within an authoritarian society, repeatedly antagonized the church and state. In the late '40s, Pasolini was charged with corrupting minors and fired from the school where he taught. He was expelled from the Communist party. In 1955, Pasolini was indicted for obscenity following the publication of his novel, *Ragazzi di vita*. This marked the first of 33 legal charges issued against the filmmaker over the next 20 years, charges he successfully defended himself against. Pasolini continually fought against the restrictions on individual freedoms instituted by the church and state.

Pasolini's entry into filmmaking was assisting Federico Fellini on the screenplay of *Nights of Cabiria* (1955). Pasolini's film work was a natural extension of his writing. His films balanced linguistic theories and Marxist social critiques. In a groundbreaking 1965 essay Pasolini said, "the act of the filmmaker is not one but double. He must first draw the image—signs (gestures, environment, dreams, memory); he must then accomplish the very work of the writer, that is, enrich this purely morphological image—sign with his personal expression. While the writer's work is aesthetic invention, that of the filmmaker is first linguistic invention, then aesthetic."

Pier Paolo Pasolini

Pasolini's early films, *Accattone* (1961)—which was adapted from his novel—and *Mamma Roma* (1962), are uncompromising, bleak studies of the tragedies of street life. *The Gospel According to St. Matthew* (1964) is a highly unconventional reinterpretation of the life, death and resurrection of Christ. His visual style was stark and simple, relying on natural light, long takes and stationary camera set-ups. With his mid- and late-'60s output *Hawks and Sparrows* (1966), *Teorema* (1968) and *Pigsty* (1969), Pasolini's work shifted significantly, away from earlier poetic naturalism to a deeply allegorical, mythic cinema concerned with symbols and representation. Historian David Cook argued in *The History of Narrative Film*, "Pasolini at his best succeeded in creating an intellectual cinema in which metaphor, myth, and narrative form all subserved materialist ideology."

Pasolini's '60s work also took on a political subtext, a reflection of his despair at the extreme social and class divisions in Italian society. In films such as *Oedipus Rex* (1967) and *Medea* (1969), Pasolini expressed a daring affinity for the neglected and abused, the marginalized, the "sub-proletariat" that migrated to the Northern cities after the Second World War. "My view of the world is always at bottom of an epical-religious nature: therefore even, in fact above all, in misery-ridden characters, characters who live outside of a historical consciousness, these epical-religious elements play a very important part."

In the '70s Pasolini unleashed his "trilogy of life," three literary adaptations of what he called the "ontology of reality" (*Decameron, Canterbury Tales, Arabian Nights*). His last film was *Salo* (1975), a shocking adaptation of Marquis de Sade's 18th-century novel *The 120 Days of Sodom*.

Pasolini was brutally murdered in 1975 by a male prostitute who ran over Pasolini's body with the director's car. The young man claimed Pasolini made compromising sexual advances and he killed the director in self-defense. Pasolini's mysterious death was the subject of a documentary film, *Whoever Tells the Truth Shall Die*, which suggests the director may have been killed by a cabal of right-wing fascists. A biography, Barth David Schwartz's *Pasolini Requiem*, was published in 1992.

Decameron

Taxi Zum Klo

T

A very funny autobiographical excursion into Berlin's gay underground. The director (Frank Ripploh) plays a sexually open teacher whose lover never wants to leave their solitary apartment. Ripploh gives into his wanderlust and drifts into the Berlin netherworld of anonymous sex with hilarious, eye-opening results. "The film succeeds on the strength of a surprising irony and wit, and a tacky exuberance that can't fail to disarm, entertain, and maybe even dispel a few myths" (*Time Out*). Cinematography by Horst Schier. With Bernd Broaderup, Magdalena Montezuma and Tabea Blumenschein. German with English subtitles.

VHS: S01304. $39.95.

Frank Ripploh, W. Germany, 1980, 94 mins.

Tchaikovsky

A panoramic, opulent biography which focuses on the life, times, art and despair of the 19th-century composer, the film centers on Tchaikovsky's antagonistic relationship with his mentor, the pianist Rubenstein, and his long-term benefactor, the Baroness von Meck. It downplays the composer's homosexuality to develop the details of his unhappy marriage. Music arranged and conducted by Dimitri Tiomkin. Cinematography by Margarita Pilikhina. With Innokenti Smoktunovsky, Antonina Shuranova and Evgeni Leonov. Russian with English subtitles.

VHS: S19056. $59.95.

Igor Talankin, Russia, 1971, 153 mins.

Tea & Sympathy

Vincente Minnelli's watered-down adaptation of Robert Anderson's play is set in a prep school where a teacher's wife tries to coax a student out of his latent gay tendencies. A victim to censorship, *Tea & Sympathy* is nevertheless interesting as an early effort of Hollywood to deal with a gay theme. With Deborah Kerr, John Kerr, Leif Erickson, Edward Andrews, Darryl Hickman and Dean Jones.

VHS: S13190. $19.98.

Vincente Minnelli, USA, 1956, 122 mins.

Teaserama: David Friedman's Roadshow Rarities: Vol. 1

A fascinating underground history on the origins of the exploitation film, showcasing the extraordinary presence of Betty Page in a collection of erotic vignettes. Betty Page performs opposite the self-named Tempest Storm, Cherry Knight, Honey Baer, Trudy Wayne and Chris La Chris.

VHS: S18439. $24.95.

Teorema

A mysterious figure (Terence Stamp) insinuates himself into the life of a wealthy industrialist (Massimo Girotti) and promptly seduces each member of the family—father, mother, son, daughter and the maid. His sudden, unexplained departure leaves each of them devastated and on the verge of madness. "The achievement of *Teorema* was to dragoon the male crotch into the realms of art, in the guise of offering a critique on the bourgeoisie" (David Shipman, *The Story of Cinema*). At the time of its release, the film was banned and Pasolini was arrested for obscenity. Cinematography by Silvana Mangano, Anne Wiazemsky, Laura Betti and Andres Jose Cruz. Italian with English subtitles.

VHS: S18193. $29.95.

Pier Paolo Pasolini, Italy, 1968, 93 mins.

The Testament of Orpheus

The final film of poet, philosopher and critic Jean Cocteau is a private diary. Together with *Orpheus* and *Blood of a Poet*, it forms a loose trilogy—a kind of intimate look at the creative process. It is full of haunting images and poetic gags as the self-named Poet (Cocteau) wanders through an 18th-century landscape, surrounded by friends, characters and figures from his earlier works. "A film, whatever it may be, is always its director's portrait" (Jean Cocteau). Cinematography by Roland Pointoizeau. Music by Georges Auric. With Edouard Dermithe, Maria Casares, Francois Perier, Yul Brynner, Pablo Picasso and Jean-Pierre Leaud. French with English subtitles.

VHS: S01313. $29.95.

Jean Cocteau, France, 1959, 80 mins.

Thank You and Goodnight

A stylish and highly original film by Jan Oxenberg that uses memory, anecdote and avant-garde representations (such as cardboard cut outs) to explore the tender, beautiful and emotionally devastating relationship between the filmmaker and her grandmother. "Wildly inventive and unique, it's a cosmic, cerebral comedy of a Woody Allenish sort" (*Toronto Globe*).

VHS: S18269. $19.98.
Jan Oxenberg, USA, 1991, 90 mins.

Therese and Isabelle

This adaptation of Violette Leduc's novel depicts the social isolation and intense erotic attraction of two young women who, liberated from their repressive girls' school atmosphere, finally acknowledge their mutual attraction on holiday. With Essy Persson, Anna Gael and Barbara Laage. English dubbed.

VHS: S01320. Currently out of print. May be available for rental in some video stores.
Radley Metzger, France, 1968, 102 mins.

These Three

William Wyler's dark adaptation of Lillian Hellman's breakthrough work *The Children's Hour*, about an unbalanced teenage girl who destroys two teachers' reputations by promulgating lies and deceptions about their private lives. Later remade by Wyler as *The Children's Hour*, which is more explicit and does not disguise the central lesbian situation. Cinematography by Gregg Toland (*Citizen Kane*). With Miriam Hopkins, Merle Oberon, Joel McCrea and Bonita Granville.

VHS: S03128. $19.98.
William Wyler, USA, 1936, 93 mins.

They Eat Scum

John Waters called this underground epic a "disgusting outlay of cheapness, decadence, nihilism and everyday cannibalism. Nick Zedd's film must rank as something of an ultimate achievement of non-committal, unblinking savagery, a true expression of what used to be called the 'punk ethos.'" With Donna Death.

VHS: S10162. $39.95.
Nick Zedd, USA, 1979, 70 mins.

This Property Is Condemned

Notable as Sydney Pollack's first collaboration with Robert Redford, this adaptation of a one-act Tennessee Williams play takes up the playwright's gothic themes of desire and temptation. Set in a mysterious Mississippi boarding house, the film concerns a sexually ambivalent woman (Natalie Wood) who must choose between a wealthy tenant (Redford) and another man. Francis Ford Coppola worked on the screenplay. Cinematography by James Wong Howe (*Sweet Smell of Success*). With Charles Bronson, Robert Blake and Kate Reid.
VHS: S04399. $19.95.
Sydney Pollack, USA, 1966, 110 mins.

This Special Friendship

French director Jean Delannoy's feature is a romantic evocation of seduction and desire, infatuation and tenderness. Set in a repressive Jesuit boarding school in France, the film explores the explosive homoerotic attractions within a group of school boys. "A masterpiece...shocking in the best sense of the word" (*Los Angeles Times*). Featuring a stunning performance by Didier Haudepin. French with English subtitles.
VHS: S01333. $49.95.
Jean Delannoy, France, 1964, 99 mins.

Three of Hearts

This is your basic love story: girl meets girl, girl loses girl, girl hires boy

Taxi Zum Klo

(played by Sherilyn Fenn), and now it has come to Fenn's moving out to protect her "space." Distraught, Lynch hires male prostitute Billy Baldwin to romance and reject Fenn, hoping to get her back on the rebound. Film was released on tape with two alternate endings: Baldwin gets the girl or Baldwin loses the girl. Losing the girl is a much better ending, but you'll have to watch to see.

VHS: S19476. $19.95.
Yurek Bogayevicz, USA, 1993, 101 mins.

Tidy Endings

An unconventional drama about the relationship between two mourners, Marion (Stockard Channing) and Arthur (Harvey Fierstein), who are grieving over the death of the same man, her former husband and his one-time lover. Rather than search out scapegoats, the two forge a tender friendship.

VHS: S09606. Currently out of print. May be available for rental in some
   video stores.
Gavin Miller, USA, 1989, 54 mins.

Tie Me Up! Tie Me Down!

Spanish provocateur Pedro Almodovar's black sexual thriller about a recently released mental patient (Antonio Banderas) who is obsessed with a soft-porn film star (Victoria Abril). When she rejects his overtures, he kidnaps her and sets in motion an intriguing emotional and sexual power play. "Almodovar's strength lies in his technical expertise and his direction of the actors, who are always able to tread the thin line between melodrama and comedy" (*The Faber Companion to Foreign Films*). Cinematography by Jose Luis Alcaine. Music by Ennio Morricone. With Loles Leon, Francisco Rabal and Julieta Serrano. Spanish with English subtitles.

VHS: S12994. $19.95.
Pedro Almodovar, Spain, 1990, 103 mins.

Time Expired

A frenetic, powerful independent short about a convict (Bob Gosse) about to be released from jail who must choose between the two loves of his life: his loyal, spirited wife (Edie Falco) and his extravagant transvestite lover (John Leguizamo).

VHS: S18969. $14.95.
Danny Leiner, USA, 1992, 30 mins.

The Times of Harvey Milk

A powerful, compassionate documentary about the political life and shocking death of Harvey Milk, San Francisco's first openly gay Supervisor, who, along with Mayor George Moscone, was assassinated by Dan White, a fired City Supervisor and political enemy. The film realistically captures the gay liberation movement in San Francisco, which encountered hostile social structures, public disapproval and institutional resistance. The portrait of Milk—assembled through interviews and archival footage—is funny and ultimately devastating. Winner of the 1984 Academy Award for Best Documentary Film.
VHS: S01348. $39.95.
Robert Epstein/Richard Schmiechen, USA, 1984, 90 mins.

To Play or To Die

Set in a Dutch boys' school, the introverted, shy Kees enters into a psychosexual battle of wills with his handsome tormentor Charel, the leader of a brutal gang that uses sadomasochistic games to assert its power. Screenplay by former Paul Verhoeven collaborator Frank Krom and Anne Van De Putte. With Geert Hunaerts and Tjebbo Gerritsma. Dutch with English subtitles.
VHS: S18587. $39.95.
Frank Krom, USA, 1991, 50 mins.

Tokyo Decadence

The gifted Japanese novelist and filmmaker Ryu Murakami adapts his novel *Topaz* in this haunting work about a prostitute's (Miho Nikaido) search for redemption. Set amid the squalor of Tokyo, Ai falls under the spell of a charismatic dominatrix and tries desperately to reverse her slide into cocaine dependency and sexual slavery. "Murakami adeptly throws us off balance, with deadpan black humor and a complex politic involving the notion of 'wealth without pride'" (Toronto Film Festival). Cinematography by Tadash Aoki. With Sayoko Amano, Tenmei Kanou and Masahiko Shimada. Japanese with English subtitles.
VHS: S19176. $29.95.
Ryu Murakami, Japan, 1991, 112 mins.

Torch Song Trilogy

Harvey Fierstein radically reshaped his important Broadway play and contributes a persuasive turn that features Arnold (Fierstein), an unreconstructed drag queen looking for emotional commitments and inner peace. The early sections concern Arnold's affairs with a

Tea & Sympathy

Thank You and Goodnight

handsome bisexual (Brian Kerwin) and a quiet, irreverent young man (Matthew Broderick). The second half showcases Anne Bancroft's bravura turn—playing the quintessential Jewish mother—as Arnold's disapproving mother. The movie is "a rollercoaster of politics, parenthood, death, independence, reconciliation and more romance. The film is a solid, old-fashioned, soppy movie and a great retro-romance" (*Time Out*).
VHS: S09390. $19.95
Paul Bogart, USA, 1988, 119 mins.

Tout Une Nuit

On a blistering hot summer night in Brussels, a parade of fanciful lovers and free spirits collide, make love, swirl and dance in a haze of incandescent fragments and vignettes. A woman leaves her husband in bed to rendezvous with her lover. A little girl runs away from home with her cat in tow. A man gazes impulsively through a window at a woman sitting alone. The film is a beautifully constructed work about small gestures and romantic longings that expands on and quietly subverts typical narrative forms. Cinematography by Carolin Champetier. With Angelo Abazoglou, Natalia Ackerman and Veronique Alain. French with English subtitles.
VHS: S12561. $29.95.
Chantal Akerman, France/Belgium, 1982, 89 mins.

Towers of Open Fire

William S. Burroughs and Brion Gysin crossed paths with Ian Sommerville and Antony Balch during their European wanderings in the late 1950s, a seminal period that witnessed the publication and attempted suppression of Burroughs' *Naked Lunch*. These films (*Towers Open Fire, The Cut-Ups, Bill & Tony* and *William Buys a Parrot*) are the cinematic equivalent of Burroughs' literature, capturing the socio-political consciousness of the period.
VHS: S09556. $19.95.
Antony Balch, USA, 1962-72, 35 mins.

Trash

A subversive companion work to Paul Morrissey's early *Flesh*, about Joe (Joe Dellesandro), a street hustler whose heroin addiction renders him impotent. "True-blue movie-making, funny and vivid...the story of Joe and his lover-protector, Holly, who is something to behold—a comic book Mother Courage who fancies herself as Marlene Dietrich but sounds more like Phil Silvers. Joe and Holly try to make a go of things in their Lower East Side basement, from which Holly goes forth from time to time to cruise the Fillmore East and scavenge garbage cans, while Joe's journeys are in search of real junk" (Vincent Canby). Produced by Andy Warhol. With Holly Woodlawn, Jane Forth and Michael Sklar.

VHS: S06251. Currently out of print. May be available for rental in some video stores.

Paul Morrissey, USA, 1970, 110 mins.

This Special Friendship

Turnabout: The Story of the Yale Puppeteers

Dan Bessie crafted this documentary about the three gay puppeteers who enchanted Hollywood for 25 years. Their musical extravaganzas drew legends like Hitchcock to see their performances with their puppet replicas of celebrities. The sophisticated humor of their shows came from a unique camp sensibility, one fostered by these three gay men in a time when being gay was extremely difficult.

VHS: S27492. $39.95.
Dan Bessie, USA, 1992, 55 mins.

Twice a Woman

The director of the chilling *The Vanishing* switches gears with this somber tale featuring Bibi Andersson and Anthony Perkins. They play a couple whose disintegrating marriage is left unresolved because of their mutual attraction for an enigmatic young woman (Sandra Dumas).

VHS: S01381. Currently out of print. May be available for rental in some video stores.
George Sluizer, Great Britain, 1985, 90 mins.

Two in Twenty

This campy lesbian soap opera follows the intersecting fates of two flamboyant households. The program deploys humor and suspense to explore the ethical and moral implications of child custody, lesbian parenting, AIDS, substance abuse, racism and coming out. The filmmakers design mock commercials for fictitious products and services that blithely satirize the extravagant consumerism of daytime television. 252 mins.

Two in Twenty: Vol. 1.
VHS: S16835. $39.95.

Two in Twenty: Vol. 2.
VHS: S16836. $39.95.

Two in Twenty: Vol. 3.
VHS: S16837. $39.95.

U Urinal

An innovative first feature, *Urinal* summons seven gay artists from 1937 and gives them an "Impossible Mission": they must research the policing of washroom sex in Ontario, and propose solutions. Each night they convene to present a lecture, with every lecture adopting a different documentary convention. Using interviews with politicians, gay activists and men who have been charged with "gross indecency," hundreds of victims of police entrapment and video surveillance are revealed. A funny and disturbing film that probes into the roots of discrimination against homosexuals. From Canada's most controversial independent filmmaker.

VHS: S15808. $39.95.

John Greyson, Canada, 1988, 100 mins.

Victor/Victoria

Varietease: David Friedman's Roadshow Rarities, Vol. 2

V

A dazzling archival study about the art and beauty of the striptease act. World champion Betty Page takes on a host of formidable rivals, including Lili St. Cyr, Chris La Chris and transvestite stripper Vicki Lynn in competition for the Anatomy Award of 1955.

VHS: S18440. $24.95.

Vegas in Space

Drag Queens bring Vegas glamour to an intergalactic battle of outsized proportions. Well, the proportions of the miniature sets are all too obvious but then so is the drag in this campy, overacted farce. An all-women planet is thrown out of whack by a dastardly crime. Two earth astronauts are sent to help, but there is one condition. They must become women to enter this feminine planet. The rest is showbiz herstory. Features the late Doris Fish.

VHS: S27624. $69.98.
Phillip R. Ford, USA, 1991, 85 mins.

Veronica Voss

The final part of Rainer Werner Fassbinder's loose trilogy on the West German "Economic Miracle" is a complicated look at the political, cultural and social repercussions of the Nazi past. A variation of Billy Wilder's cynical Hollywood masterpiece *Sunset Boulevard*, *Veronica Voss* follows the efforts of a crafty journalist (Hilmar Thate) to learn the fate of Veronica Voss (Rosel Zech)—a leading '30s film star who had a connection with Goebbels. Thate discovers that Voss is demented and under the influence of a doctor (Anne Marie Duringer) who controls her through morphine addiction. Xaver Schwarzenberger's textured black-and-white photography creates an elusive, sinister atmosphere. Music by Peer Raben. With Cornelia Froeboess, Doris Schade and Armin Mueller-Stahl. German with English subtitles.

VHS: S14808. Currently out of print. May be available for rental in some video stores.
Rainer W. Fassbinder, W. Germany, 1981, 104 mins.

A Very Natural Thing

A young priest drops out of the Church to openly pursue a gay life in New York. He falls in love with a seemingly ideal man, but together they learn that passion and romance take time. Only by learning to respect each other can their love grow. This is the first U.S. film from an openly gay director to be commercially distributed. It captures the feeing of an era when gay men were just beginning to experience greater acceptance.

VHS: S28054. $39.95.

Christopher Larkin, USA, 1973, 85 mins.

Via Appia

This is a complex work about gay desire and mounting paranoia and fear. A former German steward travels to Rio to find a mysterious man who left a cryptic message, "Welcome to the AIDS Club," following a sexual encounter. "*Via Appia*, the nickname of a Rio district where male prostitutes hang out, becomes a grim guided tour of the city's gay subculture—its bars, discos, streets and a beach known as 'The AIDS farm.' The documentary-within-the film-format justifies this material" (Vincent Canby). Cinematography by Peter Christian Neumann. Music by Charly Schoppner. With Peter Senner, Guilherme de Padua and Yves Jansen. German and Spanish with English subtitles.

VHS: S18693. $39.95.

Jochen Hick, Germany/Brazil, 1992, 90 mins.

Victim

Dirk Bogarde stars in this brooding, electrifying thriller about a closeted gay barrister who is threatened with blackmail after his lover is murdered. Despite the troubling consequences that may follow if his homosexuality is revealed, Bogarde feverishly pursues a public prosecution of the killers. The film is noteworthy for its intelligent, honest treatment of gay persecution by an intolerant culture. Written by Janet Green and John McCormick. With Sylvia Sims, Dennis Price, Nigel Stock and Peter McEnery.

VHS: S03489. Currently out of print. May be available for rental in some video stores.

Basil Dearden, Great Britain, 1961, 100 mins.

Victor/Victoria

Blake Edwards' film on sexual role playing and gender politics is a brilliant musical about an unsuccessful depression-era Paris singer (Julie Andrews) who performs as a gay female impersonator. James Garner plays a Chicago gangster whose attraction for Andrews becomes a daring subversion of male bravado. The cast includes Robert Preston as Andrews' gay mentor, a funny, heartbreaking turn by Lesley Ann Warren as a gangster's moll, and Alex Karras as Garner's gay henchman. Music by Henry Mancini.

VHS: S01412. $19.98.
Laser: LD70700. $39.98.
Blake Edwards, USA, 1982, 133 mins.

Vidal in Venice, Part One

The caustic American expatriate Gore Vidal guides the viewer through Venice's vibrant, mysterious history. Vidal covers the past and present, offering a running commentary on Venetian culture. The program includes visits to Crete and Maxos, former Venetian strongholds. 55 mins.

VHS: S05050. $29.95.

Vidal in Venice, Part Two

The second volume of Vidal's film essay on Venice explores the city's art treasures, brooding architecture, sumptuous palaces, literary tradition and scandalous past. 55 mins.

VHS: S05051. $29.95.

The Virgin Machine

Called "a lesbian *Candide*...that's deliriously obscene" by the *San Francisco Examiner*, *The Virgin Machine* is Monika Treut's offbeat study of cultural and social dislocation. The story focuses on a dissatisfied West German woman in pursuit of her mother. Her odyssey moves from Germany to San Francisco's outlandish porn district, where she encounters Susie Sexpert, a woman who lectures on the sexual politics of stripping and handles dildos with a natural aplomb. German with English subtitles.

VHS: S10940. $29.95.
Monika Treut, W. Germany, 1988, 90 mins.

A Virus Knows No Morals

Alternately irreverent and profoundly serious, the film is a savagely funny burlesque on the specter of AIDS. Nurses on the night shift roll dice to see which AIDS patient will die next. One victim is harassed by a reporter on his deathbed—he sticks her with a contaminated syringe. The government opens a quarantine called Hell Gay Land, and gay terrorists respond by kidnapping the Minister of Health. The film conjures up an outrageous and frightening landscape that violently rejects social and political norms and comments on social and political hysteria through shock humor. German with English subtitles.

VHS: S09350. $39.95.

Rosa von Praunheim, W. Germany, 1985, 82 mins.

A Virus Knows No Morals

Gus Van Sant (b. 1950) is one of the most important contemporary American independent filmmakers. He was born in Louisville, Kentucky, but moved and grew up in Darien, Connecticut. After studying film and painting at the Rhode Island School of Design, he moved to Hollywood and began an association with independent producer Ken Shapiro (*The Groove Tube*). In Los Angeles, Van Sant made a series of eccentric shorts, the most significant of which was *Alice in Hollywood*, an ironic piece about the experiences of a young, naïve actress.

Frustrated by the lack of opportunities in Hollywood, Van Sant left for New York, where he directed commercials for a Madison Avenue advertising firm. After working for two years in New York, Van Sant moved to Portland, Oregon, in the late '70s. Van Sant established a signature aesthetic that was rooted in the melancholic spaces of the Pacific Northwest. In the early '80s he made a series of compelling shorts, including *The Discipline of DE*, adapted from a William S. Burroughs short story, and *Five Ways to Kill Yourself*. In addition, Van Sant began to paint and direct music videos, and briefly taught film production at the Oregon Art Institute.

Van Sant's affinity for the poetry of the streets sets his work apart. His first feature, the 1986 *Mala Noche*, concerned a skid-row liquor clerk's unrequited obsession for an illegal Mexican worker. The film, shot in black-and-white 16mm for $25,000, was never released commercially, although it won the Los Angeles Film Critics Award for Best Independent/Experimental Feature in 1987. *Mala Noche* showcased Van Sant's highly original visual design, with its attention to space, unity and movement. In a 1991 interview, Van Sant said, "I come from painting, [where] there's a traditional arranging of objects, and my visual design probably comes from that—the arranging of forms in a pattern, and using those forms in a limited field from which to paint."

Van Sant's first art-house hit was the 1989 *Drugstore Cowboy*, which starred Matt Dillon and Kelly Lynch as a couple of thieves who rob pharmaceutical stores to support their drug habits. In 1989 the National Society of Film Critics honored the film as the year's Best Picture and Van Sant as Best Director. Van Sant's third feature, the 1991 *My Own Private Idaho*, is his most audacious—a daring revision of Shakespeare's *Henry IV Part I* within the trappings of a contemporary road movie. River Phoenix plays a gay, narcoleptic street hustler searching for his mother. Keanu Reeves is a bisexual, gilded young man, who is the son of the Portland mayor.

Gus Van Sant

Van Sant's fourth feature is *Even Cowgirls Get the Blues*, a funky adaptation of Tom Robbins' eccentric novel detailing the odyssey of a flamboyant hitchhiker, Sissy Hankshaw (Uma Thurman), who falls in with a group of renegade lesbian outlaws. The film's visual design is influenced by Kenneth Anger's *Scorpio Rising* and other important 1960s East Coast experimental filmmakers.

Van Sant's latest work is an adaptation of Joyce Maynard's novel, *To Die For*, in collaboration with writer/actor Buck Henry, and stars Matt Dillon and Nicole Kidman in an Oscar-nominated performance. Loosely based on the Pam Smart murder case, it is a campy black comedy about a social-climbing cable-access weather girl, but it is not explicitly gay. In addition to his work in features, Van Sant has directed music videos for David Bowie, Elton John, Tracy Chapman and The Red Hot Chili Peppers. He is also responsible for a collection of photography, *108 Portraits*.

Gus Van Sant, Jr.'s features are highly personal, lyrically extravagant and ambitious films from an idiosyncratic free thinker. He is an artist who literally has tried to reinvent himself each time out.

Mala Noche

Waiting for the Moon

W

Jill Godmilow's quiet, serene meditation on the artistic and emotional bonds between lovers Gertrude Stein (Linda Bassett) and Alice B. Toklas (Linda Hunt), the American expatriates who galvanized disillusioned artistic and intellectual circles in Paris' cafe society. With Andrew McCarthy as Ernest Hemingway.

VHS: S04343. Currently out of print. May be available for rental in some video stores.

Jill Godmilow, USA, 1986, 101 mins.

Waking Up: A Lesson in Love

The feature debut of documentary filmmaker Greta Schiller (*Before Stonewall*) is a piercing, emotionally honest dissection of a young woman's journey of self-exploration. The film—shot on location in Austin, Texas—is a collection of painful, funny vignettes unfolding in the casual, loose rhythms of the aggressively hip lesbian bar Petticoat Junction.

VHS: S07854. $39.95.

War Requiem

Derek Jarman's cinematic visualization of Benjamin Britten's celebrated oratorio mixes live action with documentary footage from 20th-century wars. Told as the rueful remembrance of an old soldier, the film is both a faithful and exhilarating visual manifestation of Britten's work. "Jarman wrings remarkable silent performances from [Tilda] Swinton, who embodies the awful roles traditionally allotted the female principal in war. The script subtly intertwines the poems' slight strains of a story with imagined scenes around the poet at war" (*Time Out*). With Nathaniel Parker, Laurence Olivier, Patricia Hayes and Rohan McCullough.

VHS: S13410. $29.95.

Derek Jarman, Great Britain, 1988, 92 mins.

Warm Nights on a Slow Moving Train

An off-center story about loneliness and longing, *Warm Nights on a Slow Moving Train* concerns a young woman (Wendy Hughes)—helped by a gay train steward—who travels to Sydney each weekend. There she earns money as a quietly effective prostitute. Hughes casually dons a series of elaborate guises and impersonations to service an eccentric and improbable gathering of men, in a part of the train appropriately titled the Judy Garland Suite. Cinematography by Yuri Sokol. With Colin Friels and Peter Whitford.

VHS: S10344. $19.95.
Bob Ellis, Australia, 1987, 92 mins.

We Think the World of You

An odd adaptation of Joseph R. Ackerly's novel about the uncertain relationship of a disaffected, working-class gay man (Alan Bates) and his distant, jailed lover (Gary Oldman). Bates gathers a peculiar strength from his imprisoned lover's family, especially his prized Alsatian. The movie is a work of subtle gestures about the consequences of unrequited love. With a dynamic performance by Oldman as the gruff bisexual lover. With Frances Barber, Liz Smith and Max Wall. Adaptation by Hugh Stoddart.

VHS: S09208. Currently out of print. May be available for rent in some video stores.
Colin Gregg, USA, 1988, 94 mins.

We Were One Man

Set during World War II, *We Were One Man* is the story of an obsessive relationship between a simple-minded French farmer and an abandoned, wounded German soldier. Guy, the strong and energetic farmer, unconsciously seduces Rolf, the susceptible, blond warrior. Winner of the Silver Hugo at the 1980 Chicago Film Festival. "A seductive, tightly written little gem" (Mark Hallek, *New York Native*). "Vallois eloquently conveys the claustrophobic emotions of his characters, and draws superb performances" (*The Faber Companion to Foreign Films*). Cinematography by Francois About. With Serge Avedikian, Piotr Stanislas and Catherine Albin. French with English subtitles.

VHS: S01437. $49.95.
Philippe Vallois, France, 1980, 90 mins.

West Coast Crones:
A Glimpse into the Lives of Nine Old Lesbians

A touching and revealing documentary about the relationships among nine aging women as they confront severe changes in their lives and reflect on and candidly discuss their lives and the consequences of getting old. An honest, heartfelt film work that subverts stereotypes.

VHS: S16832. $39.95.

Madeline Muir, USA, 1991, 28 mins.

What Have I Done to Deserve This?

In Pedro Almodovar's farce, an assortment of strange grotesques hover around the crowded Madrid apartment of a working-class couple. Gloria (Carmen Maura) is a disaffected housewife and Antonio (Angel De Andres-Lopez) is her brutish husband. Antonio seduces a middle-aged writer (Gonzalo Suarez), setting in motion a violent series of events, including blackmail, extortion and murder. The film is "an absolutely wonderful black comedy. A small masterpiece" (*The New York Times*). Cinematography by Jose Luis Martinez. With Luis Hostalot, Veronica Forque and Juan Martinez. Spanish with English subtitles.

VHS: S08102. $79.95.

Pedro Almodovar, Spain, 1985, 100 mins.

Whatever Happened to Susan Jane?

This low-budget comedy moves from New York's Lower East Side to San Francisco's psychedelic underground. A bored East Coast housewife pursues a former high school classmate, a shy loner named Susan Jane. She finds, to her considerable surprise, that Susan Jane frequents San Francisco's netherworld of punks, transvestites, artists and bohemians. With Ann Black, Francesca Rosa and Lulu. Music from San Francisco's underground scene, including Tuxedomoon, Indoor Life and the Wasp Women.

VHS: S02347. Currently out of print. May be available for rental in some video stores.

Mark Huestis, USA, 1984, 60 mins.

White Nights

Luchino Visconti's adaptation of Dostoevsky's short story details the complicated emotional relations between a poor, determined man (Marcello Mastroianni) who falls for an enigmatic woman (Maria Schell) who is awaiting the return of her missing lover (Jean Marais). Visconti shifts the setting to contemporary Livorno, and creates a visually spare, theatrical space. Cinematography by Giuseppe Rotunno. Music by Nino Rota. With Clara Calamai. Italian with English subtitles.

VHS: S13679. $59.95.
Luchino Visconti, Italy, 1957, 107 mins.

Whoever Says the Truth Shall Die

This remarkable film depicts the life and violent death of poet, political theorist and filmmaker Pier Paolo Pasolini. The film works on two levels: first, as a fascinating biographical look at Pasolini and his career, and secondly, as an investigation into the possibility that Pasolini was assassinated by a group of right-wing fascists rather than killed by a 17-year-old male prostitute. Includes interviews with actress Laura Betti and director Bernardo Bertolucci. English and Italian with English subtitles.

VHS: S02654. $59.95.
Philo Bregstein, Holland, 1981, 60 mins.

Wild Blade

Five wildly disparate people are all attracted to a young male prostitute (Stephen Geoffreys) whose married trick died under mysterious circumstances. The dead man's wife, a pimp and a jealous lover all conspire and negotiate for possession of the hustler. With Sheila Kelley, Carole Scott, Thom Crouch and Geoffrey Paltrowitz. Cinematography by Joseph Piazzo.

VHS: S18588. $29.95.
David Geffner, USA, 1992

Wild Life

John Goss' video portrait of two 15-year-old gay Los Angeles Latinos combines documentary-style interviews with fictional segments as they act out their elaborate fantasies. A work about transformation, the director views them changing into "wild style," cruising around "Gay City," casually hanging with their friends at the park and "throwing attitude." They discuss the implications of being gay and

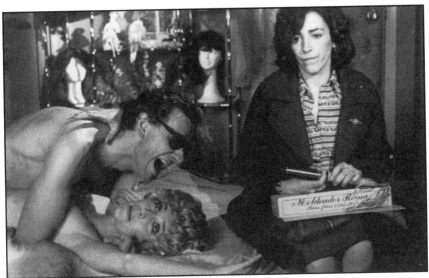
What Have I Done to Deserve This?

their relationships with friends and lovers.
VHS: S06509. $49.95.
John C. Goss, USA, 1985, 40 mins.

The Wild Party

Adapted from a narrative poem by Joseph Moncure March, James Ivory's film is a portrait of decadent lesbians, gay piano players and the unbridled hedonism of Hollywood in the 1920s. The film stars James Coco as a Fatty Arbuckle-like comedian who orchestrates a grand party to restore his self-destructive career. With Raquel Welch, Perry King, Tiffany Bolling, David Dukes and Royal Dano.
VHS: S03898. Currently out of print. May be available for rental in some video stores.
James Ivory, USA, 1975, 107 mins.

Wild Reeds

In 1962, a group of teenagers confront emotional, sexual and political turmoil provoked by both their own personal lives and the larger social framework of a small provincial town impacted by the French-Algerian War. This engaging, elegaic film captures both the fleeting nature of youth and the profound turmoil of this intriguing stage of life. French with English subtitles.
VHS: S29407. $89.98.
Andre Techine, France, 1995, 110 mins.

We Were One Man

Wild World of Lydia Lunch

An intimate, no-holds-barred portrait of the no-wave rocker and bawdy exhibitionist Lydia Lunch. The film contains the short *Thrust in Me*, with director Nick Zedd playing transsexual roles in collaboration with cinematographer Richard Kern (*Kiss Me Goodbye* and *Go to Hell*.)
VHS: S10164. $39.95.
Nick Zedd, USA, 1983-86, 61 mins.

William S. Burroughs:
Commissioner of the Sewers

A portrait of the revolutionary author who created the epic *Naked Lunch*. With his characteristic deadpan wit and droll humor, Burroughs discusses language, death and dreams, and the scientific concerns of travelling through time and space. Burroughs reads from his works and talks about his paintings and films.
VHS: S16621. $29.95.
Klaus Maeck, USA, 1986, 60 mins.

Window Shopping

Chantal Akerman's dazzling riff on earlier French musicals deals with the romantic fortunes of cheerful shopkeepers and workers at an antiseptic shopping mall. The characters are consumed with love and romance, issues which lead to interesting gossip at the local hair dressing salon. "A feminist director of often minimalist and low-key films, Akerman has turned her hand to a musical in which the themes of love, sex and commerce are closely linked. If the undertones are

bittersweet and sometimes cynical, the surface glints diamond bright" (*The Faber Companion to Foreign Films*). Cinematography by Gilberto Azevedo and Luc Benhamou. With Delphine Seyrig, Myriam Boyer, Fanny Cottencon and Lio. French with English subtitles.
VHS: S13820. $29.95.
Chantal Akerman, France/Belgium, 1986, 96 mins.

Withnail and I

Bruce Robinson's quixotic and mournful film about the end of the 1960s is an autobiographical treatment about two vociferously independent roommates and London actors whose grim existence is enlivened by the pleasures of a friend's country estate. "Robinson's debut exhibits the values of the old virtues: characterization, detail and engagement, none more so than the elephantine figure of Richard Griffiths as Withnail's gay uncle. It's a true original" (*Time Out*). With Richard E. Grant, Paul McGann and Michael Elphick.
VHS: S07577. $14.95.
Laser: LD71214. $49.95.
Bruce Robinson, Great Britain, 1988, 108 mins.

Without You I'm Nothing

Sandra Bernhard's adaptation of her off-Broadway show is a stylized, documentary-like examination of the nature of performance, identity and the culture of celebrity. In a brilliant dialectic on the relationship of performer and audience, Bernhard seamlessly inhabits various roles and personalities to make pungent and hilarious comments about music, art, fashion, politics and sex. With John Doe, Steve Antin and Cynthia Bailey.
VHS: S13266. $19.98.
John Boskovich, USA, 1990, 90 mins.

A Woman in Flames

A sensation when it was released, *A Woman in Flames* is a sexual thriller about a woman who abandons her suffocating marriage and turns to prostitution. She meets and befriends a male hustler, though the relationship is eventually undermined by her sexual jealousies. *A Woman in Flames* is a trenchant critique of sex, class and power. Cinematography by Jurgen Jurges. Music by Peer Raben. With Gudrun Landgrebe, Mathieu Carriere and Hanns Zischler. English dubbed.
VHS: S01474. Currently out of print. May be available for rental in some video stores.
Robert van Ackeren, W. Germany, 1984, 106 mins.

Women from Down Under

Australian and New Zealand directors made these lesbian shorts. Italian food, Bulgarian folksinging, truckers and the morning after are just some of the surprising elements that come up in these entertaining works. Included are *Peach, Just Desserts, Excursion to the Bridge of Friendship* and *Jumpin' the Gun*. 52 mins.
VHS: S27609. $29.95.

Women on the Verge of a Nervous Breakdown

Pedro Almodovar's breakthrough film is his most assured work, blending his affinity for pop farce and social observations with his anarchic sensibility. In the madcap plot, an insecure television actress (Carmen Maura) is abandoned by her lover after he discovers she is pregnant. Her attempts to reach him are continually thwarted by a surreal chain of events. "What lingers in the memory [is]...scenes of a Wilder-like sophistication dotted with improbable props, action, inflated campery, and most of Almodovar's usual repertory-style company" (*Time Out*). Cinematography by Jose Luis Alcaine. With Antonio Banderas, Fernando Guillen, Julieta Serrano and Maria Barranco. Spanish with English subtitles.
VHS: S10757. $19.98.
Pedro Almodovar, Spain, 1988, 89 mins.

Word Is Out: Stories of Some of Our Lives

From the director of *Absolutely Positive*, this is a landmark effort to assess gay identity. Twenty-six men and women ranging in age from 18 to 77 speak about their experiences of being gay in a homophobic America, in what Vito Russo in *The Advocate* called "an electric piece of living history." The result is a poignant look at often courageous lives revealed in stories that are alternately moving, funny and bitterly real. *Word Is Out* was the first major film to explore America's gay culture.
VHS: S16077. $29.95.
Peter Adair, USA, 1977, 130 mins.

The World According to Garp

George Roy Hill's adaptation of John Irving's novel interweaves the political and sexual. The hero is Garp (Robin Williams), the bastard son of Jenny Fields (Glenn Close)—a pioneering feminist whose break-the-rules manner gives the film its free form. From its ironic opening, scored to The Beatles' "When I'm 64," *Garp* is a darkly comic succession of vignettes about life, death and resurrection. John Lithgow is hilarious as Roberto Muldoon, a transsexual and former pro football player who became disillusioned with masculine behavior. Cinematography by Miroslav Ondricek. Written by playwright Steve Tesich (*Breaking Away*). With Mary Beth Hurt, Hume Cronyn, Jessica Tandy, Swoosie Kurtz and Amanda Plummer.

VHS: S04472. $19.98.
George Roy Hill, USA, 1982, 136 mins.

World & Time Enough

Winner of the Audience Award, San Francisco Lesbian & Gay Festival, this is a "...gentle, enchanting comic drama" (*OUT Magazine*) about gay love in which a mellow garbageman and found-object collector, Joey (Gregory G. Giles), and an HIV-positive artist/provocateur, Mark (Matt Guidry), work at maintaining a monogamous relationship. Debut film by Minneapolis director Eric Mueller. "...a '90s *Parting Glances*...leaves its pushy, big-budget mainstream kin like *Jeffrey* in their own archaic haze, still mincing and miserable" (*The Village Voice*).

VHS: S30137. $39.99.
Eric Mueller, USA, 1996, 92 mins.

WR: Mysteries of the Organism

Dusan Makavejev's landmark film deftly juxtaposes the story of a sexual encounter between the beautiful, liberated Milena and a repressed Soviet figure-skating champion. *WR* is a meditation on the life and theories of the Austrian psychoanalyst Wilhelm Reich, who revolutionized theories of sexual liberation and social repression. Makavejev describes the film as "a black comedy, political circus, a fantasy on the fascism and communism of human bodies, the political life of human genitals, a proclamation of the pornographic essence of any system of authority and power over others.... If you watch for more than five minutes, you become my accomplice." Jackie Curtis appears in a major section. Cinematography by Pega Popovic and Aleksandar Petkovic. With Milena Dravic, Jagoda Kaloper and Tuli Kupferberg. English and Serbian with English subtitles.

VHS: S11290. $79.95.
Dusan Makavejev, Yugoslavia/USA, 1971, 84 min.

Y

You Are Not Alone

A provocative Danish film about two boys at a Danish boarding school who, in the middle of a student strike, find themselves strongly attracted to each other. A "gentle and funny" (*Seattle Times*) story of budding sexuality, *You Are Not Alone* is reminiscent of the early films of Truffaut. Danish with English subtitles.

VHS: S01491. $79.95.

Lasse Nielsen, Denmark, 1982, 90 mins.

Young Hearts, Broken Dreams, Episode 1: The Delivery Boy

Eddie Starr and Mark Cannon star in one of the first gay soap operas, the ongoing saga of a troubled gay movie star, his lover, his friends, sex, drugs, Hollywood and life in the fast lane. Adam Harrington, a delivery boy at Paramount Pictures, finds all his romantic longings fulfilled when he meets and moves in with his idol, gay movie star Scottie Edwards. Unfortunately, Scottie is beholden to a ruthless drug lord, and he and Adam decide to skip town together. In the end, however, they must face reality and return to the oversexed world of gay Hollywood.

VHS: S27722. $49.95.

Gerald Gordon, USA, 1990, 45 mins.

Young Hearts, Broken Dreams, Episode 2: The Search

After the disastrous outcome of the first episode, an entirely new cast of characters comes to the foreground in this steamy sequel. Scottie Edwards' brother Matthew and his best friend Noah leave Nebraska to come to Hollywood and avenge Scottie's death. Before long, Matt realizes that he's falling for Zech, the handsome detective assigned to Scottie's murder. *The Search* continues the exciting mix of sex, sensuality, and emotional ups and downs found in the first episode of this soap opera. Michael Habusch and Robert Spiewak star.

VHS: S27723. $59.95.

Gerald Gordon, USA, 1995, 83 mins.

Zazie dans le Metro

Z

An anarchic comedy about peculiar family dynamics captures a tense 36-hour period when a foul-mouthed 11-year-old teams up with her reluctant female impersonator uncle to experience the wonder and joy of early '60s Paris. It's "an exceedingly funny picture...in a bold, delicate, freakish, vulgar, outrageous, and occasionally nightmarish way. The picture is crammed with sight gags and preposterous photographic stunts. *Zazie* is a film like *Alice in Wonderland*; nobody and nothing are quite what they seem" (Pauline Kael). Cinematography by Henri Raichi. With Catherine Demongeot, Philippe Noiret, Carla Marlier and Vittorio Caprioli. French with English subtitles.

VHS: S12991. $29.95.

Louis Malle, France, 1960, 85 mins.

You Are Not Alone

A leading figure in postwar Italian cinema, **Luchino Visconti** (1906-76) was born in Milan into a prominent aristocratic family. Visconti was educated at private schools in Milan and Como and went on to serve in a cavalry regiment in the late '20s. He was initially attracted to the theater. He worked as the set designer for theater director G.A. Traversi, while also acting in several small roles. In 1936, Visconti moved to Paris and worked as a costume designer and assistant director with Jean Renoir on two films, *The Lower Depths* (1936) and *A Day in the Country* (1936),

before returning to Italy with Renoir to make *La Tosca* (1940). Renoir abandoned the project because of the outbreak of World War II, and the film was eventually completed by his assistant, Carl Koch.

Visconti's debut film, *Ossessione* (1942), is considered by many film historians to be a founding moment in the history of Italian neorealism. His next film, *La Terra Trema* (1947), a loose adaptation of Sicilian novelist Giovanni Verga's *Il Malavoglio*, incorporated the key formal devices of neorealism: location shooting, the use of non-actors, improvised dialogue, long takes and naturalistic lighting. Visconti shared, along with seminal neorealist directors Roberto Rossellini and Vittorio De Sica and writer Cesare Zavattini, a set of moral and political commitments and the belief the cinema could serve as a catalyst for social change. Neorealism was in decline by the early '50s, in part because of government censorship and export restrictions.

Bellissima (1951) marked the beginning of Visconti's shift from neorealism to the melodramatic, operatic style of his middle and late period works. With *Senso* (1954), Visconti challenged the heroic myths of the Risorgimento, the 19th-century movement for Italian unity. Discussing the film, Visconti said, "The idea was to use history as a backdrop for the personal story of Countess Serpieri, who was ultimately no more than the representative of a certain social class. What I was interested in was the story of a bungled war, a war waged by a single class and ending in fiasco." Film historian Robert Phillip Kolker contends that "*Senso* established [Visconti's] approach—his decadence, if you will—manifested in his need to pump his *mise-en-scene* and stuff the cinematic space he creates with opulent detail that overwhelms the characters, who in turn overwhelm themselves with melodrama."

Luchino Visconti

In the '50s Visconti directed his first opera, *La Vestale*, and also worked on the production of two ballets, *Mario e il Mago* and *Maratona di danza*. Aside from the 1960 *Rocco and His Brothers*— a partial return to neorealist tendencies—the remainder of Visconti's work consisted of the lavish historical dramas and stylized literary adaptations *White Nights* (1957), *The Leopard* (1963), *Death in Venice* (1971) and *The Innocent* (1973). In a critical essay evaluating his career, Andrew Sarris wrote, "Visconti himself was like the protagonist in a Visconti movie: trapped by the contradictions of his personality, aware of social injustice but too faithful to the documentation of luxury to caricature the upper classes.... Like most accomplished directors, Visconti became more intuitively confessional as he got older. Ultimately, he came out of many closets. He never seemed to lose his power to outrage the critical establishment."

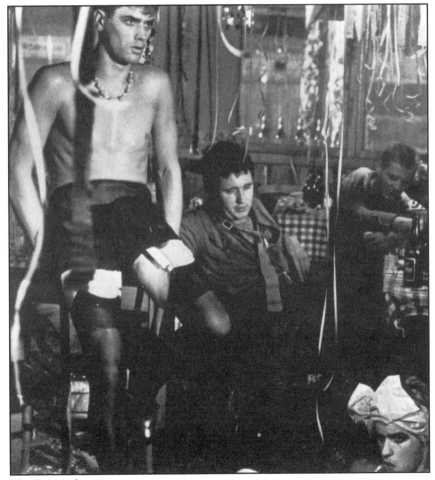

The Damned

AIDS and Health-Related Instructional and Educational Video

Asi Me Gusta

Latino men offer perspectives on family, "coming out," substance abuse and gay identity. 18 mins.
VHS: S28418. $15.00.

Clean Needles Save Lives

This video documents the illegal efforts of militant activists with ACT-UP and their needle exchange program in New York. The program combines interviews with recovering drug users discussing how to reduce risk and incorporate safer sex practices. 28 mins.
VHS: S18775. $20.00.

Current Flow

Taken from the popular work *Safer Sex Shorts*, this explicit sexual program demonstrates safer sex practices for sexually active gay women. 5 minutes.
VHS: S18776. $15.00.

Da Vinci Body Series: Vol. 1

Subtitled *A Workout for the Renaissance Man of the '90s*, this program takes the viewer through rigorous movements, exercises and routines to explore the best means to achieve maximum strength and conditioning for the upper body. With a step-by-step narration.
VHS: S18260. $24.95.

Da Vinci Body Series: Vol. 4

Subtitled *Stretch*, seven fully nude male athletes demonstrate Eastern techniques of body stretching for a sharper mind, a more supple physique and a drive to conquer all challenges. 42 mins.
VHS: S30138. $24.95.

Doctors, Liars and Women: AIDS Activists Say "No" to Cosmo

In January 1988, a group of women from ACT-UP organized a protest against *Cosmopolitan Magazine* for publishing an article that gave seriously misleading information to women about AIDS. *Doctors, Liars and Women* documents the process of organizing AIDS activists around issues pertinent to women. Produced by the Gay Men's Health Crisis. 23 mins.
VHS: S11424. $19.95.

Edith Springer on Harm Reduction

Edith Springer provides insight on how harm reduction has worked in her training of street youth peer educators in New York City, in this humorous, fast-paced training video. 26 mins.
VHS: S28414. $25.00.

Encuentro Sin Riesgo—Safer Encounter

A brand new and explicit video specifically targeted to gay men, starring Latin porn sensation Freddie Mac. The video includes safer oral sex, safer anal sex, masturbation, a condom demonstration, and tips on how to have safer erotic sex. The information is presented in Spanish and in English. Produced by Gay Men's Health Crisis. 14 mins.
VHS: S19484. $15.00

Fear of Disclosure

Phil Zwickler and David Wojnarowicz explore the psychological and social implications of informing a potential lover one is HIV-positive. 5 minutes.

VHS: S18777. $10.00.

Fit!

A landmark exercise video launched by and for gay men, this rigorous exercise program studies the relationship of aerobics and stress reduction movements on the immune system. The program combines a cardiovascular workout with the tenets of yoga and relaxation. The workout is supervised and choreographed by Jon Griswold, an internationally renowned trainer. 50 mins.

VHS: S18261. $29.95.

An Informed Approach to HIV Antibody Testing

An informative and sensitive video that considers the personal and social consequences of testing. From the Gay Men's Health Crisis' *Living with AIDS* cable program. 22 mins.

VHS: S18774. $25.00.

Invisible Women

A group of Latina women explore their personal enlightenment through education, art and activism, confronting previously held ideas and attitudes about AIDS. Three women describe their personal experiences of being HIV-positive. Produced by Phil Zwickler and Jonathan Lee. 26 mins.

VHS: S18778. Currently out of print. May be available for rental in some video stores.

"It Is What It Is"

An important educational video that discusses teen sexuality, HIV prevention and social isolation, the program is split into three 20-minute segments: *Identity*, which concerns the social and personal dislocation teens experience in expressing their sexuality, whether straight or gay; *Homophobia*, which reveals options for teens confronting anti-gay and lesbian sentiments, particularly the fear of AIDS; and *Safer Sex*, which deals with safe sex practices, abstinence, the specter of HIV, sexually transmitted diseases and pregnancy. The program is accompanied by a discussion guide that lays out lesson plans and instructs teachers on developing classroom discussions. "This is the first AIDS education video I've seen that realistically addresses the complex issue of teen sexuality, coming out and AIDS" (Reverend Margaret A. Reinfeld, American Foundation for AIDS Research). 60 mins.
VHS: S18781. $50.00.

Living Proof

A divergent group of lesbians and gay men recovering from alcohol and drug addictions speak about the issues related to their communities regarding substance abuse and HIV status. 28 mins.
VHS: S18779. $50.00.

Memento Mori

This hand-processed, 16mm Cinemascope meditation on death by Jim Hubbard contrasts the four seasons with the scattering of a person's ashes in the Seine.
VHS: S28579. $59.95.

"Non, Je Ne Regrette Rien" (No regrets)

Through music, poetry, and quiet self-disclosure, five HIV-positive, black gay men speak of their individual confrontations with AIDS, illuminating the difficult journey black men throughout America make in coping with the personal and social devastation of the epidemic. Directed by Emmy Award-winner Marlon Riggs. 42 mins.
VHS: S19449. Currently out of print. May be available for rental in some video stores.

Nude Stretching

You haven't experienced the full pleasure of stretching until you have seen these exercises and practiced them in the nude with this fully instructional stretching tape. 45 mins.
VHS: S30134. $19.98

Nude Tai Chi

Whether to learn the many benefits of this art, or to simply enjoy the beauty of the naked human form, viewers will find many hours of enjoyment that energizes the body, soothes the mind, and delights the spirit in this fully instructional tape. 40 mins.
VHS: S30133. $19.98

Prostitutes, Risk and AIDS

Prostitutes are frequently scapegoated as the vectors of HIV transmission. This fallacy is often based upon prejudices that evolve out of stereotypical representations in media. This videotape provides an analysis of these images in the context of sex workers and health care professionals who are actively educating the public about safer sex and IV drug use. Produced by the Gay Men's Health Crisis. 28 mins.
VHS: S11425. $19.95.

PWA Power

A diverse group of people with AIDS/ARC talk about their experiences, offering valuable insights to those recently diagnosed with AIDS. First-person accounts about the birth of the PWA self-empowerment movement are included. Produced by the Gay Men's Health Crisis.
VHS: S11426. $25.00.

Safer Sex Shorts

You can have hot sex without placing yourself at risk for AIDS (or other STD's)! A series of erotic and explicit "shorts" combine the driving rhythm of music videos with slick, rapidly edited images; scenarios include *Something Fierce*, a condom demonstration; *Midnight Snack*, featuring oral sex; *Car Service*, making it in the back seat; *Current Flow*, safer sex for women who have sex with women; and *Law and Order*, with some serious S/M. Produced by the Gay Men's Health Crisis. 25 mins.
VHS: S11427. $50.00.

Same Stuff, Different Day

An intergenerational discussion on gay identity, community, substance use, HIV and AIDS is presented in this collaboration with Gay Men of African Descent. 20 mins.
VHS: S28417. $15.00.

See for Yourself

Jerry Tartaglia employs a formalist syntax to create an intimate and moving document of a friend dying from AIDS, in this silent film.
VHS: S28582. $59.95.

Seize Control of the FDA

On October 11, 1988, at 7:00 a.m., hundreds of AIDS activists from around the U.S. seized control of the offices of the Food and Drug Administration in Rockville, Maryland. This tape documents the events and addresses the issues that motivated this non-violent direct action. Produced by the Gay Men's Health Crisis. 28 mins.
VHS: S11428. $19.95.

Steps Toward Change

Four individuals speak about their experiences as participants of Substance Use & Counseling Education's (SUCE) ongoing peer education group for HIV-positive gay men. 20 mins.
VHS: S28416. $15.00.

Talk About It

Six HIV-negative or untested gay men speak candidly about isolation, oral sex and other issues related to remaining HIV-free. 19 mins.
VHS: S28415. $15.00.

A Test of the Nation

AIDS impacts on many of the problems facing women, children and families in America today. This videotape addresses the larger issues of reproductive rights, access to quality health care and the standard of living for many women and children in our society. Produced by the Gay Men's Health Crisis. 28 mins.
VHS: S11422. $19.95.

Thinking About Death

This program reflects on death, mortality, isolation and loss from multiple perspectives in dealing with the specter of AIDS/HIV and the effects on one's companions, family and friends. 28 mins.
VHS: S18780. $50.00.

Voices from the Front

Shot across North America and Britain, this documentary explains both the rationale and the causes espoused by a generation of AIDS activists. This tape offers a singular opportunity to hear from activists themselves about the nature of their work. It was all about ending the AIDS crises, which despite the efforts of so many, became a worldwide epidemic.
VHS: S27911. $39.98.

Walt Odets on Primary Prevention for Gay Men

Nationally recognized psychologist Walt Odets, author of *In the Shadow of the Epidemic: Being HIV-Negative in the Age of AIDS*, is interviewed in this training video for counselors. 27 mins.
VHS: S28413. $25.00.

Women and AIDS

"Women take care of everyone; who takes care of women?" Although women have been dying of AIDS since 1981, little attention has been paid to their particular situation. *Women and AIDS* explores the underlying issues of how AIDS highlights problems such as racism, sexism, child care and lack of adequate health care for women. Produced by the Gay Men's Health Crisis. 28 mins.
VHS: S11430. $25.00.

Work Your Body

The purpose of this video is to help those who are HIV-positive, asymptomatic or otherwise, to develop strategies for living with HIV infection. Strategies for pursuing prophylactic treatments and diligently maintaining one's health are discussed. Produced by the Gay Men's Health Crisis. 28 mins.
VHS: S11431. $25.00.

Additional Gay & Lesbian Videos and Laser Discs

The following films available on video and laser disc have a more marginal gay or lesbian content which ranges from secondary gay or lesbian characters to often stereotypical or homophobic portrayals of homosexuality.

After Hours
Martin Scorsese, USA, 1985, 97
  mins.
VHS: S00021. $19.98.

American Gigolo
Paul Schrader, USA, 1980, 117
  mins.
VHS: S10017. $14.95.

Barbarella
Roger Vadim, France, 1968, 98
  mins.
VHS: S00095. $19.95.

Bedazzled
Stanley Donen, Great Britain, 1967,
  107 mins.
VHS: Out of print. May be available for
  rental in some stores.
Laser: LD70867. $59.95.

Beverly Hills Cop
Martin Brest, USA, 1984, 105 mins.
VHS: S01839. $19.95.

Beyond the Valley of the Dolls
Russ Meyer, USA, 1979, 123 mins.
VHS: S18599. $19.98.

Billy Budd
Peter Ustinov, Great Britain, 1962,
  123 mins.
VHS: S01690. $59.98.

Broadway Melody 1929
Harry Beaumont, USA, 1929, 104
 mins.
VHS: S08337. $19.98.

California Suite
Herbert Ross, USA, 1978, 103 mins.
VHS: S10374. $19.95.

Camille
George Cukor, USA, 1937, 110 mins.
VHS: S03453. $24.95.

Car Wash
Michael Schultz, USA, 1976, 97
 mins.
VHS: S07800. Currently out of print.
 May be available for rental in some
 stores.

Choirboys
Robert Aldrich, USA, 1977, 120
 mins.
VHS: S10450. $14.98.

Cleopatra Jones
Jack Starrett, USA, 1973, 89 mins.
VHS: S18927. $19.98.

Day of the Locust
John Schlesinger, USA, 1975, 140
 mins.
VHS: S10824. $14.95.

Day of the Jackal
Fred Zinnemann, Great Britain/
 France,1973, 143 mins.
VHS: S07808: $59.95.

Day for Night
Francois Truffaut, France, 1973, 116
 mins.
VHS: S00308. $59.95.

Deathtrap
Sidney Lumet, USA, 1976, 116 mins.
VHS: S04333. $69.95.

Detective
Robert Hamer, Great Britain, 1954,
 91 mins.
VHS: S07584. $19.95.

Diamonds Are Forever
Guy Hamilton, USA, 1971, 119
 mins.
VHS: S00337. $14.98.

Down and Out in Beverly Hills
Paul Mazursky, USA, 1986, 103
 mins.
VHS: S00362. $19.95.

Dracula's Daughter
Lambert Hillyer, USA, 1936, 70
 mins.
VHS: S17272. $14.98.

Eiger Sanction
Clint Eastwood, USA, 1975, 125
 mins.
Laser: LD70292. $39.98.

Evil Under the Sun
Guy Hamilton, Great Britain, 1982,
 117 mins.
VHS: S04545. $19.99.

Fame
Alan Parker, USA, 1980, 133 mins.
VHS: S05952. $19.98.

Farewell, My Lovely
Dick Richards, Great Britain, 1975,
 95 mins.
VHS: S02144. $19.95.

Five Easy Pieces
Bob Rafelson, USA, 1970, 96 mins.
VHS: S07789. $14.95.

From Russia with Love
Terence Young, Great Britain, 1963,
 118 mins.
VHS: S05015. $14.98.

Funny Lady
Herbert Ross, USA, 1975, 137 mins.
VHS: S05095. $14.95.

Garbo Talks
Sidney Lumet, USA, 1985, 104 mins.
VHS: S15250. $19.98.

Gay Divorcee
Mark Sandrich, USA, 1934, 107
mins.
VHS: S03268. $19.98.

Hospital
Arthur Hiller, USA, 1971, 102 mins.
VHS: S15251. $19.98.

Inside Daisy Clover
Robert Mulligan, USA, 1965, 128
mins.
VHS: S15935. $19.98.

Justine
George Cukor, USA, 1969, 115 mins.
VHS: S02324. $59.98.

La Dolce Vita
Federico Fellini, Italy, 1961, 180
mins.
VHS: S00705. $24.95.

The Last Metro
Francois Truffaut, France, 1980, 135
mins.
VHS: S00724. $29.95.
Laser: LD71522. $69.95.

The Lion in Winter
Anthony Harvey, Great Britain,
1968, 135 mins.
VHS: S01796. Currently out of print.
May be available for rental in some
stores.

Lisztomania
Ken Russell, Great Britain, 1975,
105 mins.
VHS: S00759. $19.98.

Little Big Man
Arthur Penn, USA, 1970, 147 mis.
VHS: S07721. Currently out of print.
May be available for rental in some
stores.

Live and Let Die
Guy Hamilton, Great Britain, 1973,
121 mins.
VHS: S07310. $19.95.

Lord Jim
Richard Brooks, Great Britain,
1965, 154 mins.
VHS: S01711. $19.95.

The Lost Weekend
Billy Wilder, USA, 1945, 100 mins.
VHS: S06869. $19.95.

Magic Christian
Joseph McGrath, Great Britain,
1970, 88 mins.
VHS: S04244. $14.98.

Mahogany
Berry Gordy, USA, 1976, 109 mins.
VHS: S10831. $14.95.

The Man Who Fell to Earth
Nicolas Roeg, Great Britain, 1976,
140 mins.
VHS: S00815. $69.95.

Merry Christmas, Mr. Lawrence
Nagisa Oshima, Japan/Australia,
1983, 124 mins.
VHS: S00850. Currently out of print.
May be available for rental in some
stores.

Midnight Express
Alan Parker, USA, 1978, 123 mins.
VHS: S02549. $69.95.

Missouri Breaks
Arthur Penn, USA, 1976, 127 mins.
VHS: S03622. $19.98.

Mona Lisa
Neil Jordan, Great Britain, 1986,
104 mins.
VHS: S03294. $14.95.

Myra Breckinridge
Michael Sarne, USA, 1970, 94 mins.
VHS: Out of print for some time. Rental
copies in stores are difficult to find.

Next Stop Greenwich Village
Paul Mazursky, USA, 1976, 109
mins.
VHS: S16686. $59.98.

Old Dark House
James Whale, USA, 1932, 71 mins.
VHS: S16180. $24.95.

One Flew over the Cuckoo's Nest
Milos Forman, USA, 1975, 129 mins.
VHS: S18973. $14.98.

Papillon
Franklin Schaffner, USA, 1973, 150
mins.
VHS: S10936. $19.98.

Pawnbroker
Sidney Lumet, USA, 1965, 116 mins.
VHS: S01004. $19.98.

Performance
Nicolas Roeg and Donald Cammell,
Great Britain, 1968, 110 mins.
VHS: S01009. $19.98.

Persona
Ingmar Bergman, Sweden, 1966, 81
mins.
VHS: S17865. $19.98.

Pete 'n' Tillie
Martin Ritt, USA, 1972, 100 mins.
VHS: S10799. $19.98.

The Producers
Mel Brooks, USA, 1968, 88 mins.
VHS: S01064. Currently out of print.
May be available for rental in some
stores.

Queen Christina
Robert Mamoulian, USA, 1933, 97
mins.
VHS: S11732. $19.98.
Laser: LD70661. $29.98.

Radio Days
Woody Allen, USA, 1987, 89 mins.
VHS: S04132. Currently out of print.
May be available for rental in some
stores.

Road Warrior
George Miller, Australia, 1983, 94
mins.
VHS: S01801. $14.95.
Laser: LD70739. $29.98.

Rose
Mark Rydell, USA, 1979, 134 mins.
VHS: S05622. $19.98.

Scarecrow
Jerry Schatzberg, USA, 1973, 115
mins.
VHS: S08720. $19.98.

Separate Peace
Larry Peerce, USA, 1973, 104 mins.
VHS: S05003. $49.95.

Single White Female
Barbet Schroeder, USA, 1992, 107
mins.
VHS: S18007. $19.95.

Star!
Robert Wise, USA, 1968, 194 mins.
VHS: S19485. $89.98.

**The Taking of Pelham One-Two-
Three**
Joseph Sargent, USA, 1974, 104
mins.
VHS: S17974. $14.95.
Laser: LD71177. $34.98.

Tootsie
Sydney Pollack, USA, 1982, 116 mins.
VHS: S04218. Currently out of print. May be available for rental in some stores.
Laser: LD70765. $124.95.

Tough Guys
Jeff Kanew, USA, 1986, 104 mins.
Laser: LD71374. $36.99.

Valley of the Dolls
Mark Robson, USA, 1967, 123 mins.
VHS: S18598. Currently out of print. May be available for rental in some stores.

Victim
Basil Dearden, Great Britain, 1961, 100 mins.
VHS: S03489. Currently out of print. May be available for rental in some stores.

Villain
Hal Needham, USA, 1979, 89 mins.
VHS: S17032. $19.95.

Walk on the Wild Side
Edward Dmytryk, USA, 1962, 114 mins.
VHS: S07337. $69.95.

Wild Party (1929)
Dorothy Arzner, USA, 1929, 76 mins.
VHS: S16175. $29.95.

Women in Love
Ken Russell, Great Britain, 1970, 129 mins.
VHS: S01479. $19.98.

X, Y & Zee
Brian Hutton, Great Britain, 1972, 110 mins.
VHS: S05623. Currently out of print. May be available for rental in some stores.

The Year of Living Dangerously
Peter Weir, Australia/USA, 1982, 115 mins.
VHS: S01486. $19.98.
Laser: LD70715. $34.98.

Z
Costa-Gavras, France, 1969, 128 mins.
VHS: S01496. Currently out of print. May be available for rental in some stores.

Director Index

Adair, Peter
Word Is Out: Stories of
  Some of Our Lives

Adlon, Percy
Celeste
Salmonberries

Akerman, Chantal
Akermania, Volume One
The Eighties
Je, Tu, Il, Elle
News fom Home
Tout Une Nuit
Window Shopping

Almendros, Nestor
Improper Conduct

Almodovar, Pedro
Dark Habits
Flower of My Secret
High Heels
Labyrinth of Passion
Law of Desire
Matador
Pepi, Luci, Bom and
  Other Girls on the Heap
Tie Me Up! Tie Me Down!
What Have I Done to Deserve This?

Women on the Verge of
  a Nervous Breakdown
Altman, Robert
Beyond Therapy
Come Back to the Five and Dime,
  Jimmy Dean, Jimmy Dean
Streamers

Andreff, Christine
Excursion (in *Women from Down
  Under*)

Anger, Kenneth
Fireworks
Inauguration of the Pleasure Dome
Lucifer Rising
Scorpio Rising

Araki, Gregg
The Living End

Asquith, Anthony
The Importance of Being Earnest

Attenborough, Richard
A Chorus Line

Aubert, Elisabeth
Drawing the Line: A Portrait of
  Keith Haring

Austin, Lisa
Breaking Ground (in *Strange Fruit*)

Austin, Rodney O'Neal
Pop Tarts Come in One Size
  (in *Strange Fruit*)

Avnet, Jon
Fried Green Tomatoes

Babenco, Hector
Kiss of the Spider Woman
Pixote

Balch, Antony
Towers of Open Fire

Bannert, Walter
The Inheritors

Barreto, Bruno
Amor Bandido
Happily Ever After

Barrett, Ruth
Images: A Lesbian Love Story

Bartel, Paul
Lust in the Dust
Scenes from the Class Struggle
  in Beverly Hills

Bashore, Juliet
Kamikaze Hearts

Beaudin, Jean
Being at Home with Claude

Bemberg, Maria Luisa
I the Worst of All

Benner, Richard
Outrageous

Benson, Allen
David Hockney: Portrait of an Artist

Bergman, Ingmar
Silence

Berle, Milton
Milton Berle Invites You to
  a Night at La Cage

Bertolucci, Bernardo
The Conformist
The Last Emperor

Bessie, Dan
Turnabout: The Story of
  the Yale Puppeteers

Blakemore, Michael
Privates on Parade

Blier, Bertrand
Ménage

Bogart, Paul
Torch Song Trilogy

Bogayevicz, Yurek
Three of Hearts

Boll, Christopher
Der Sprinter

Boskovich, John
Without You I'm Nothing

Bowser, Kenneth
In a Shallow Grave

Branagh, Kenneth
Peter's Friends

Brass, Tinto
Caligula

Bregstein, Philo
Whoever Says the Truth Shall Die

Bresson, Arthur J.
Abuse

Brocka, Lino
Fight for Us
Macho Dancer

Brookner, Howard
Bloodhounds of Broadway
Burroughs

Brooks, Richard
Cat on a Hot Tin Roof (1958)

Broughton, James
Autobiographical Mysteries (Testa-
  ment, Devotions, Scattered Remains)
Dreamwood
Erotic Celebrations (The Bed, Erogeny,
  Hermes Bird, Song of the Godbody)
Parables of Wonder (High Kukus,
  Golden Positions, This Is It,
  The Gardener of Eden, Water Circle)

The Pleasure Garden
Rituals of Play (Mother's Day,
    Four in the Afternoon, Loony Tom)

Camarda, George
Miguel Ma Belle (in *Boys in Love*)

Campbell, Dick
Glitter Goddess of the Sunset Strip

Campbell, Stephen
The Jim Bailey Experience

Carpi, Fabio
Basileus Quartet

Carr, Shan
Out for Laughs

Carter, Chad
Ataxiaflagris (in *Strange Fruit*)

Casner, Howard
A Cold Coming

Castle, Nick
Mr. Wrong

Cates, Gilbert
Consenting Adult

Cavani, Liliana
Berlin Affair

Chabrol, Claude
Les Biches

Chereau, Patrice
L'Homme Blesse (The Wounded Man)

Chionglo, Mel
Midnight Dancers

Clarke, Shirley
Portrait of Jason

Cocteau, Jean
Beauty and the Beast
Blood of a Poet
Jean Cocteau: Autobiography
  of an Unknown
Orpheus
The Testament of Orpheus

Compton, Joyce
Lesbionage

Conn, Nicole
Claire of the Moon
Cynara

Cronenberg, David
Naked Lunch

Dakota, Reno
American Fabulous

Dallamano, Massimo
Dorian Gray

Daniels, Alan
The Boys of Cellblock Q

Danielsson, Tage
Adventures of Picasso

Dash, Julie
Daughters of the Dust

de Koenigsberg, Paula
Rate It X

de la Iglesia, Eloy
Colegas
El Diputado
Los Placeres Ocultos (Hidden Plea-
  sures)
Navajeros (Dulces Navajas)

de Lussanet, Paul
The Dear Boys

Dearden, Basil
Victim

Deitch, Donna
Desert Hearts

Delannoy, Jean
Eternal Return
This Special Friendship

des Roziers, Hugues
Blue Jeans

Deval, Jacques
Club des Femmes

Dillinger, James
Blonde Death

Dlugacz, Judy
The Changer: A Record of the Times

Donohoe, Gerald
27 Pieces of Me

Donovan, Martin
Apartment Zero

Ebersol, P. David
Death in Venice, CA (in *Boys in Love*)

Edel, Uli
Last Exit to Brooklyn

Edwards, Blake
Victor/Victoria

Egoyan, Atom
The Adjuster

Ellis, Bob
Warm Nights on a Slow Moving Train

Epstein, Rob
Celluloid Closet
Common Threads: Stories from the
    Quilt
The Times of Harvey Milk

Erman, John
An Early Frost

Evans, Kim
Andy Warhol

Fassbinder, Rainer W.
Ali: Fear Eats the Soul
The American Soldier
The Bitter Tears of Petra Von Kant
Chinese Roulette
Despair
Fox and His Friends
Gods of the Plague
I Only Want You to Love Me (Ich Will
    Doch Nur, Dass Ihr Mich Liebt)
The Marriage of Maria Braun
The Merchant of Four Seasons
Mother Kusters Goes to Heaven
Querelle
Stationmaster's Wife
Veronica Voss

Fellini, Federico
Fellini Satyricon

Feret, Rene
The Mystery of Alexina

Finch, Nigel
The Lost Language of the Cranes

FitzGerald, Jon
Apart from Hugh

Ford, Phillip R.
Vegas in Space

Fosse, Bob
Cabaret

Foster, Jodie
Home for the Holidays

Frears, Stephen
My Beautiful Laundrette
Prick Up Your Ears
Sammy and Rosie Get Laid

Friedkin, William
Boys in the Band
Cruising

Friedman, Jeffrey
Celluloid Closet
Common Threads: Stories from the
    Quilt

Fukasuku, Kinjki
Black Lizard

Gabrea, Radu
A Man Like Eva

Gardan, Juliusz
Is Lucyna a Girl?
    (Czy Lucyna to Dziewczyna?)

Gasper, Mark
Empty Bed

Gates, Jim
Milton Berle Invites You to
    a Night at La Cage

Gauthier, Paula
Le Poisson de Amour (in *I Became a
    Lesbian and Others Too*)

Geffner, David
Wild Blade

Genji, Nakamura
Beautiful Mystery

Gisler, Marcel
The Blue Hour

Glenville, Peter
Becket

Godmilow, Jill
Waiting for the Moon

Gold, Jack
The Naked Civil Servant

Gordon, Gerald
Young Hearts, Broken Dreams,
   Episode 1: The Delivery Boy
Young Hearts, Broken Dreams,
   Episode 2: The Search

Goss, John
Out Takes
Stiff Sheets
Wild Life

Gregg, Colin
We Think the World of You

Greyson, John
Urinal

Guttman, Amos
Drifting

Hammer, Barbara
Lesbian Humor (Menses, Superdyke,
   Our Trip, Sync Touch, Doll House,
   No No Nooky TV)
Lesbian Sexuality (Dyketactics,
   Multiple Orgasm, Double Strength,
   Women I Love)
Optical Nerves (Optic Nerve,
   Place Mattes, Endangered)
Perceptual Landscapes (Pools, Pond
   and Waterfall, Stone Circles, Bent
   Time)

Hampton, Christopher
Carrington

Handelman, Michelle
BloodSisters

Hansen, Dane
Mine Eyes Have Seen the Glory:
   The Women's Army Corps

Hansen, Ellen J.
Moments: The Making of
   Claire of the Moon

Harrison, Hugh
Dream Man
Jerker
On Common Ground

Harrison, John Kent
Beautiful Dreamers

Harron, Mary
I Shot Andy Warhol

Hart, Harvey
Fortune and Men's Eyes

Haynes, Todd
Poison

Hazan, Jack
A Bigger Splash

Hemmings, David
Just a Gigolo

Henszelman, Stefan Christian
Friends Forever

Herbert, Henry
Forbidden Passion

Hermosillo, Jaime H.
Dona Herlinda and Her Son

Hershey, Ann
Imogen Cunningham: Never Give Up

Hick, Jochen
Via Appia

Hickox, Douglas
Entertaining Mr. Sloane

Hill, George Roy
The World According to Garp

Hiller, Arthur
Making Love

Hiroyuki, Oki
I Like You, I Like You Very Much

Hitchcock, Alfred
Rope

Hofsiss, Jack
Cat on a Hot Tin Roof (1984)

Huestis, Marc
Men in Love
Whatever Happened to Susan Jane?

Hughes, Kelly
La Cage aux Zombies

Huston, John
The Night of the Iguana
Reflections in a Golden Eye

Ivory, James
Maurice
The Wild Party

Jarman, Derek
The Angelic Conversation
Caravaggio
Edward II
Jubilee
The Last of England
Louise (from Aria)
Sebastiane
War Requiem

Jimenez-Leal, Orlando
Improper Conduct

Johnson, Jed
Andy Warhol's Bad

Jones, Marvin
Love Bites

Jordan, Glenn
A Streetcar Named Desire

Jordan, Neil
The Crying Game

Julien, Isaac
Looking for Langston

Jutra, Claude
By Design

Kaczender, George
Chanel Solitaire

Kalin, Tom
Swoon

Kaneko, Shusuke
Summer Vacation: 1999

Kanievska, Marek
Another Country

Kaufman, Philip
Henry & June

Kazan, Elia
Baby Doll
A Streetcar Named Desire

Keith, Harvey
Mondo New York

Kessler, Bruce
Gay Deceivers

Klaus, Veronica
How Long Must I Wait for You?
  (in *Strange Fruit*)

Kleiser, Randal
It's My Party

Krom, Frank
To Play or To Die

Kubrick, Stanley
Spartacus

Kuchar, George
Indian Summer (in *Strange Fruit*)

Kumel, Harry
Daughters of Darkness

Kureishi, Hanif
London Kills Me

Kurys, Diane
Entre Nous

LaBruce, Bruce
No Skin off My Ass

Larkin, Christopher
A Very Natural Thing

Lautner, Georges
La Cage aux Folles III: The Wedding

Lauzon, Jean-Claude
Night Zoo

Lean, David
Lawrence of Arabia

Leiner, Danny
Time Expired

Lester, Richard
The Ritz

Levey, William A.
Monaco Forever

Lewin, Albert
The Picture of Dorian Gray

Lindsay-Hogg, Michael
As Is

Litten, Peter
The Art of Cruising Men

Livingston, Jennie
Paris Is Burning

Losey, Joseph
La Truite (The Trout)
Romantic Englishwoman
The Servant
Steaming

MacDonald, Heather
Ballot Measure 9

Mackenzie Litten, Peter
Heaven's a Drag

Maeck, Klaus
William S. Burroughs:
  Commissioner of the Sewers

Makavejev, Dusan
WR: Mysteries of the Orgnism

Makin, Kelly
Brain Candy

Makk, Karoly
Another Way

Malle, Louis
Zazie dans le Metro

Mankiewicz, Joseph L.
Suddenly, Last Summer

Marshall, Stuart
Desire

Masenza, Claudio
Rebels: Montgomery Clift

McLaughlin, Sheila
She Must Be Seeing Things

Medak, Peter
The Krays

Metzger, Radley
Therese and Isabelle

Mikesch, Elfi
Seduction: The Cruel Woman

Miller, Claude
The Best Way

Miller, Gavin
Tidy Endings

Minnelli, Vincente
Tea & Sympathy

Molinaro, Edouard
La Cage aux Folles
La Cage aux Folles II

Moriarty, John
Dream Boys Revue

Morrissey, Paul
Andy Warhol's Dracula
Andy Warhol's Frankenstein
Beethoven's Nephew
Flesh
Heat
Mixed Blood
Spike of Bensonhurst
Trash

Mueller, Eric
World & Time Enough

Muir, Madeline
West Coast Crones: A Glimpse into
  the Lives of Nine Old Lesbians

Munch, Christopher
The Hours and Times

Murakami, Ryu
Tokyo Decadence

Narizzano, Silvio
Loot

Newman, Paul
The Glass Menagerie

Nichols, Mike
The Birdcage
Silkwood

Nielsen, Lasse
You Are Not Alone

Noonan, Chris
Cass

Onodera, Midi
A Performance by Jack Smith

Osten, Suzanne
The Mozart Brothers

Oxenberg, Jan
Thank You and Goodnight

Pabst, G.W.
Pandora's Box

Palazzolo, Tom
Costumes in Review
Gay for a Day

Paradjanov, Sergei
Ashik Kerib
The Color of Pomegranates
   (Director's Cut)
Shadows of Forgotten Ancestors

Parker, Christine
Peach (in *Women from Down Under*)

Pasolini, Pier Paolo
Accatone
Arabian Nights
The Canterbury Tales
Decameron
The Gospel According to St. Matthew
Love Meetings (Comizi d'Amore)
Hawks and Sparrows
Medea
Notes for an African Orestes
Oedipus Rex
Pigsty
Salo: 120 Days of Sodom
Teorema

Pierson, Frank
Citizen Cohn

Pirro, Mark
Curse of the Queerwolf

Polanski, Roman
Fearless Vampire Killers or: Pardon
   Me, But Your Teeth Are in My Neck

Pollack, Sydney
This Property Is Condemned

Pool, Lea
Straight for the Heart

Preminger, Otto
Advise and Consent

Purdue, Holly
Behnd the Door (in *Strange Fruit*)

Purves, Barry
Achilles (in *Boys in Love*)

Rafelson, Bob
Black Widow

Rappaport, Mark
The Impostors

Reid, Frances
The Changer: A Record of the Times

Rene, Norman
Longtime Companion

Ripploh, Frank
Taxi Zum Klo

Risi, Marco
Forever Mary

Rivette, Jacques
The Nun (La Religieuse)

Robinson, Bruce
Withnail and I

Rosenberg, Robert
Before Stonewall

Ross, Herbert
Nijinsky

Rossen, Robert
Lilith

Rozema, Patricia
I've Heard the Mermaids Singing

Russell, Ken
The Devils
Gothic
The Music Lovers
Salome's Last Dance

Sagan, Leontine
Maedchen in Uniform

Salva, Victor
Powder

Samperi, Salvatore
Ernesto

Saville, Philip
Shadey

Sayles, John
Lianna

Schaffner, Franklin J.
The Best Man

Schepisi, Fred
The Devil's Playground

Schiller, Greta
Before Stonewall

Schlesinger, John
Darling
An Englishman Abroad
Midnight Cowboy
Sunday Bloody Sunday

Schlondorff, Volker
Coup de Grace

Schmid, Daniel
Shadow of Angels (Schatten der Engel)

Schmidt, Richard
1988

Schmiechen, Richard
The Times of Harvey Milk

Schneider, Jane
Jumping the Gun (in *Women from Down Under*)

Schrader, Paul
Mishima: A Life in Four Chapters

Schwartz, Howard
Dream Boys Revue

Scola, Ettore
A Special Day

Shafer, Dirk
Man of the Year

Sharman, Jim
The Rocky Horror Picture Show

Sherwood, Bill
Parting Glances

Simoneau, Yves
Blind Trust

Sluizer, George
Twice a Woman

Smith, Cynthia
Images: A Lesbian Love Story

Smith, John N.
The Boys of St. Vincent

Spielberg, Steven
The Color Purple

Stevens, David
The Clinic

Stigliano, Roger
Fun Down There

Strick, Joseph
The Balcony

Sutherland, David
Paul Cadmus: Enfant Terrible at 80

Swords, Sarah
Siren

Szabo, Istvan
Colonel Redl

Talankin, Igor
Tchaikovsky

Taylor, Amanda
Cat Nyp (in *I Became a Lesbian and Others Too*)

Techine, Andre
Wild Reeds

Temple, Julien
Rigoletto (from *Aria*)

Terracino
My Polish Waiter (in *Boys in Love*)

Thornhill, Michael
Everlasting Secret Family

Topor, Roland
Marquis

Towne, Robert
Personal Best

Treut, Monika
My Father Is Coming
Seduction: The Cruel Woman
The Virgin Machine

Tsukerman, Slava
Liquid Sky

Vadim, Roger
Blood and Roses

Vallois, Philippe
We Were One Man

van Ackeren, Robert
A Woman in Flames

Van Sant, Gus
Drugstore Cowboy
My Own Private Idaho

Verhoeven, Paul
The 4th Man
Spetters

Verow, Todd
Frisk

Villaronga, Augustin
In a Glass Cage

Visconti, Luchino
Bellissima
Conversation Piece
The Damned
Death in Venice
The Innocent
La Terra Trema
Ossessione
Rocco and His Brothers
Senso
White Nights

von Praunheim, Rosa
Anita, Dances of Vice
Positive (Positiv)
Silence = Death
A Virus Knows No Morals

von Sternberg, Josef
Morocco

Walker, Nancy
Can't Stop the Music

Waters, John
Desperate Living
Female Trouble
Hairspray
Mondo Trasho
Multiple Maniacs
Pink Flamingos
Polyester

Watson, James
Lot in Sodom
    (in *American Avant-Garde Films*)

Webber, Melville
Lot in Sodom
    (in *American Avant-Garde Films*)

Weber, Bruce
Broken Noses

Wedley, Louise
Just a Little Crush (in *I Became a*
    Lesbian and Others Too)

Weill, Claudia
Girl Friends

Wertmuller, Lina
Sotto, Sotto

Winer, Lucy
Rate It X
Silent Pioneers

Woodcock, Peter
Babette in "The Return of
    the Secret Society"
Dominique in "Daughters of Lesbos"

Workman, Chuck
Superstar: The Life and Times
    of Andy Warhol

Wyler, William
The Children's Hour
These Three

Xhonneux, Henri
Marquis

Yates, Peter
The Dresser

Young, Robert M.
Short Eyes

Yu Kan-Ping
The Outcasts

Zedd, Nick
Geek Maggot Bingo
They Eat Scum
Wild World of Lydia Lunch

Zetterling, Mai
Scrubbers

Free Updates to the Facets Gay & Lesbian Video Guide

Keep up with the expanding world of gay and lesbian film on video with a *free* subscription to *Facets Alternative Lifestyle Video* newsletter. Published four times each year, the newsletter describes the dozens of new lesbian and gay video titles which become available each month. To subscribe, mail or fax the coupon below:

— —

To: **Facets Video**, 1517 West Fullerton Avenue, Chicago, IL 60614
      fax: 773-929-5437; e-mail: sales@facets.org

Enter my *free* subscription to *Facets Alternative Lifestyle Video* newsletter. I would prefer to receive the newsletter (check one)
☐   by mail   ☐   by fax   ☐   by e-mail

Name _____

Address _____

City _____   State ____   Zip _____

fax: _____

e-mail: _____